THE FESTIVAL SHAKESPEARE

*Troilus and Cressida*

# THE FESTIVAL SHAKESPEARE

# Troilus and Cressida

## The New York Shakespeare Festival Series

*Bernard Beckerman and Joseph Papp, Editors*

With an essay on the direction of the play

by JOSEPH PAPP

THE MACMILLAN COMPANY, NEW YORK

COLLIER-MACMILLAN LIMITED, LONDON

Library of Congress Catalog Card Number: 67-15048

*First Printing*

The Macmillan Company, New York
Collier-Macmillan Canada Ltd., Toronto, Ontario
PRINTED IN THE UNITED STATES OF AMERICA

# Contents

# Preface to the New York Shakespeare Festival Series

Every presentation of a Shakespearean play is a unique event in a continuing tradition. The event is unique because each production must confront the play as though it had never before been staged. A theatrical company must "forget," as it were, that it is presenting a play written by Shakespeare before it can tap the full power of his imagination. And yet, each production is still but one in the continuing tradition of exploring the seemingly infinite prospects of Shakespeare's world. In the crucible of rehearsal, each cast rediscovers the play, adding its own sensibilities to the accumulated vision of the work.

The present series is a record of such rediscoveries by the New York Shakespeare Festival. It consists of separate volumes of Shakespearean plays produced by the Festival. An historical introduction provides the critical and theatrical background against which the director's statement can be viewed. Throughout the series stress has been placed upon each director's statement, for in each case it reflects the outlook that guided the production. Photographs and production notes, indicated by asterisks in the text, offer specific illustrations of the manner in which the director's approach was expressed concretely. A complete text of the play, marked

with parentheses to indicate stage cuts, enables the
reader to compare the full copy with the performed
copy. Though each volume reflects the concerns of a
particular production, the series as a whole conveys
the spirit animating the New York Shakespeare Festival.

From its beginnings in 1953, when it was founded by
Joseph Papp, the guiding policy of the Festival has been
to provide a theater for all regardless of ability to pay.
During the summer of 1956, the Shakespeare Workshop, as the forerunner of the Festival was then called,
presented its first season of Free-Shakespeare-in-the-Park
at the East River Amphitheater in lower Manhattan. In
1957, the summer season opened at Belvedere Lake in
Central Park, continued with a tour of the five bor-
oughs, and, when the truck carrying stage and company
broke down, terminated in Central Park. For a time in
1959 the principle of free performance appeared to be
in jeopardy. The Parks Commissioner insisted that, if
performances were to be given in the park, admission
must be charged. After a series of legal contests, however, the Appellate Court upheld the Shakespeare
Workshop and the way was paved for expansion of the
Festival.

In 1959 the Board of Estimate of the City of New
York appropriated funds for the construction of a permanent amphitheater at Belvedere Lake. When these
funds proved insufficient, they were supplemented by
George T. Delacorte. Stability was further assured in
1960, when the Board of Regents of the State of New
York granted an absolute charter to the newly named
New York Shakespeare Festival. Finally, with the opening of the 2,300-seat Delacorte Theater on June 19,
1962, the Festival achieved permanency and continuity.

At the same time that it was consolidating its position
in the center of Manhattan, the Festival extended its

influence throughout the rest of the city. Commencing in 1960, the Board of Education underwrote annual tours of the New York City schools by one of the Festival productions. In 1964 the Festival initiated summer tours of city parks and playgrounds by a Mobile Unit. To reach a still broader segment of the population, the tours included plays in Spanish as well as in English. At last, in 1966, with the acquisition of the former Astor Library as a permanent home and indoor theater, the New York Shakespeare Festival established itself as a year-round theater.

The Festival itself is in the tradition of the folk or popular theater of Europe. The right of attendance by all citizens is unequivocally established, and so the audiences represent a cross section of the urban populace. The integrity of production is maintained and the plays are presented without condescension. The premise is that the best of drama can be communicated clearly and effectively as spontaneous experience, not archaic curiosity. Perhaps it is not sheer coincidence that the Delacorte Theater has many features in common with Shakespeare's Globe: an open stage, an unroofed amphitheater, an ample capacity. Nor may it be coincidence that the Festival relies so much upon touring, just as Shakespeare and his fellows did. Both the structure of the theater and the practice of touring may be essential conditions for the vigorous interplay between citizenry and performer so necessary to a healthy theater and integral to the purposes of the New York Shakespeare Festival.

*The Editors*

# The History of the Play

### ✍ *by Bernard Beckerman*

In 1623 two men were engaged upon a task that was
to earn them the gratitude of history. John Heminges
and Henry Condell, actors and partners in the leading
theatrical company, the King's men, were assembling a
complete collection of Shakespeare's works. "To keepe
the memory of so worthy a Friend, & Fellow alive," they
were determined to make available in a reliable edition
the best copy of his plays that they could provide. All
the plays were to be gathered into an impressive volume
of folio size, a dimension reserved for works of serious
literature. Eighteen of the plays included in this First
Folio had been printed in one form or another before
Heminges and Condell undertook their task.[1] Some of
these earlier editions were satisfactory; most, however,
did not do justice to the work of their former colleague.
Moreover, eighteen plays not hitherto published were
to be printed for the first time. This alone was enough
to crown their efforts. *Julius Caesar, As You Like It,*

[1] Actually nineteen plays were published in quarto by 1623.
However, *Pericles,* though attributed to Shakespeare on the
title page of the 1609 Quarto, was not included in the First
Folio by Heminges and Condell. Altogether there were six
quarto editions of this play before it was printed in the Third
Folio (1664). Today, scholars accept *Pericles* as substantially
the work of Shakespeare.

*Antony and Cleopatra, Macbeth* were among the plays salvaged from oblivion.

The Folio publication did not follow a chronological arrangement. As befitted a work of literature, the volume was subdivided by genre: first came the Comedies, then the Histories, and lastly the Tragedies. Some difficult choices had to be made, for Shakespeare had not written his plays to fit one category or another neatly. But the arrangement on the whole was well managed. Plays on English history were numbered among the histories and plays on ancient history, Greek or Roman, were placed among the tragedies—except for one play. As copy for *Troilus and Cressida* was being set by the printer, the work had to be interrupted. From what we can deduce from the scanty evidence, a dispute arose over the publishers' authority to include the play in the Folio, and so the printing of *Troilus and Cressida* did not go forward. However, rather than discontinue preparation of the entire volume, type was set for the succeeding plays. Perhaps the publishers were not certain that they would ever be able to proceed with the printing of *Troilus and Cressida*. At least they made no provision for including the play, for it is not listed in the "Catalogue of the severall Comedies, Histories, and Tragedies contained in [the] Volume." Yet somehow the obstacles that arose in securing rights to the script were overcome. Copy was set, and the play was printed, although too late for inclusion in one of the three sections of the Folio. Instead, the work was inserted between the histories and the tragedies. Fortunately the manner of the insertion reveals a glimpse of history. The title on the first page of the text and the running title on the next two pages bear the designation *The Tragedie of Troylus and Cressida*. Pagination clearly shows that the editors intended to have this play follow

6    The Festival Shakespeare *Troilus and Cressida Romeo and Juliet* in order.[2] But when printing was resumed, the running title "tragedie" and numerical designation of pages were discontinued. So there is *Troilus and Cressida*, occupying an anomalous position in the canon.

This anomaly of 1623 was not the first to beset the play. Twenty years earlier the record of its strange history begins, and that record, too, includes an interrupted printing and an uncertain past. On February 7, 1603, a copy of *Troilus and Cressida*, "as yt is acted by my lord Chamberlens Men," was entered upon the Register of the Stationers' Company, the body of printers and book sellers which monopolized the printing and publishing affairs of the city of London. Though listed, the play was not immediately printed, however, and we hear little of it at that time.

The period was one of tumultuous events for England and for the theater. A new order was soon to come to court and country. England's great Queen was failing. On March 24, 1603, Elizabeth died. Her cousin King James VI of Scotland came to the throne, and became the first of that name on the English throne. The accession of the new monarch affected the social status of the players, for the Lord Chamberlain's men were taken under the patronage of the King himself, to be known thereafter as His Majesty's Servants. Prestigious as the patronage was, it merely reflected the professional status that Shakespeare and his fellows had already achieved

[2] The final pages of *Romeo and Juliet* are numbered 76 and 79; the first pages of *Troilus and Cressida*, unnumbered, unnumbered, 79, 80. Apparently the original pagination was 76, 77 for *Romeo and Juliet*, title page of *Troilus and Cressida*, then 79 and 80. To accommodate the pagination after the removal of *Troilus and Cressida*, page 77 of *Romeo and Juliet* became page 79 and the title page of *Timon of Athens* started on page 80.

under Elizabeth. For nearly ten years Shakespeare, the great actor Burbage, Heminges, Condell, and other of their partners had struggled to achieve a preeminent position in the theatrical profession. Their principal rivals, the Lord Admiral's men and the Lord Worcester's men (after 1603, the Prince's men and Queen's men respectively), by then had been matched or surpassed. For his partners, Shakespeare had already turned out a flood of pleasant comedies, all but one of the histories, and had created four tragedies of which *Hamlet* was the latest.

But there was another sort of rivalry. Since the turn of the century, performances by acting companies of young boys had been revived after a period of fifteen or sixteen years. Because the performances were indoors, because they included some of the features of the court masque, principally dancing and singing, and because they treated provocative subjects, these performances gained an immediate popularity, enough to discomfit the adult players temporarily. Being given indoors in what was known as private theaters, the performances were more expensive, drawing a smaller and, inevitably, a more select audience. Being reflective of court style, they were also reflective of court interests. And finally, seeking to be provocative, they tended to deal with satiric materials and to adopt a sardonic tone. Inevitably the most important children's companies ran afoul of the sensitivities of the court and by 1610 were harassed or suppressed.

On January 28, 1609, *Troilus and Cressida* was again listed in the Stationers' Register, this time as a history. Whereas formerly it had been entered as the copy, that is, property of James Roberts, on this occasion it was entered as the copy of Richard Bonian and Henry Walley. Within the year the new publishers

proceeded to have a quarto edition of the play printed.
But as though to foreshadow the events of 1623, the
printing was interrupted. For some reason, which has
been fascinating to imagine but impossible to ascertain,
the wording of the title page was altered and a preface
was added. That done, the printing continued. However, since it was the practice of sixteenth-century
printers not to discard uncorrected pages but rather to
bind them with corrected pages, *Troilus and Cressida*
was issued in two different states. Some copies of the
play contained the earlier title page, some the later.
Scholars distinguish between these copies by referring
to the first and second states or issues of the 1609
Quarto.

On the title page of the first state, after the words
*The Historie of Troylus and Cresseida*, there appeared
the subscription, "As it was acted by the Kings Maj-
esties Servants at the Globe." Though this statement
may indicate that the play was performed after the Lord
Chamberlain's men were taken under royal patronage,
it may also refer to the presentation cited in the initial
entry of the play into the Stationers' Register. On the
title page of the second state, the play is called *The
Famous Historie of Troylus and Cresseid*. The subscription recommends the amatory portions of the play to
the prospective purchaser: "Excellently expressing the
beginning of their loves, with the conceited wooing of
Pandarus Prince of Licia." The preface to the reader
commended the play to the discriminating, averred that
it never had been "clapperclawed" by the public at
large, and praised highly the contents of the work. In
this preface the play is distinctly termed a comedy.[3]

---

[3] For the text of the preface to the 1609 Quarto, see Ap-
pendix.

An intriguing story no doubt lies behind the confusing history of the publications, but it is unlikely that it will ever be completely unraveled. Yet who is not tempted to reconcile the contradictory bits of evidence? When was the play written? Did it receive a performance in Shakespeare's day, and if so, where? Why did it have such a checkered publishing career? And from a critical consideration, is it indeed a history, a comedy, or a tragedy? Even in Shakespeare's own day there seems to have been disagreement on this point.

That Shakespeare and his fellow actors owned a play called *Troilus and Cressida* before 1603 is quite established. Most likely it was Shakespeare's own play though his name is not connected with it in the Register. Most likely this play was presented publicly, as the registration of 1603 states. By 1609 the same company still possessed a play called *Troilus and Cressida,* this time definitely Shakespeare's, for his name appears on the title page. In substance this play is almost certainly the same as the one listed in 1603. During the intervening years the author may very well have revised the script. The addition or deletion of some speeches or scenes might have justified a new listing. But what can we conclude from the fact that the initial title page of the 1609 edition was altered and a preface added? It seems that at first the publishers believed the play to have been performed at the Globe, then discovered that the version they possessed had never been presented publicly. Perhaps it is true, as others have argued, that the text as they had it was performed not at the Globe but before a private audience at one of the Inns of Court, those rather permissive law schools of the time. Such a performance, given sometime between 1603 and 1609, imperfectly recorded, would have led the publishers to make their initial claim and then reverse

themselves. If they could not advertise that the King's
men had performed the work, they would advertise
quite the opposite, that the play had not been sullied
by the many but had been reserved for the select few.

Another unusual aspect of the printed editions concerns the description of *Troilus and Cressida* variously
as a history, a comedy, and a tragedy. Generic classification, it is true, was never rigid in Shakespeare's day.
*Richard III* is termed a tragedy in the quarto editions
and listed as a history in the folio. On the title page of
the 1608 Quarto, *King Lear* is a "Chronicle Historie,"
and in the First Folio, a tragedy. *The Merchant of
Venice* is listed variously as a history, a comedy, or a
comical history. This overlapping between history and
either tragedy or comedy was fairly common. But
*Troilus and Cressida*, alone of Shakespeare's works, is
shifted from genre to genre as though his contemporaries did not know how to categorize the work.

After 1609 there is no reference to the play until the
First Folio is published in 1623. Thereafter, it is not
mentioned until it serves as the foundation for John
Dryden's adaptation in 1679. Dryden's Preface to his
*Troilus and Cressida* anticipates two centuries of critical
response. "Because the play was Shakespeare's, and that
there appeared in some places of it the admirable genius
of the author, I undertook to remove that heap of
rubbish under which many excellent thoughts lay wholly
buried." He was so successful in his cleanup that his
*Troilus and Cressida* continued to be performed until
1734. Meanwhile, Shakespeare's play remained in its
printed state, esteemed for speeches or characters, but
not highly considered as a finished work. Critics gave it
a sidelong glance as though they were looking at a
crippled creature. Samuel Johnson thought it a play in
which neither "the extent of [Shakespeare's] views or
elevation of his fancy is fully displayed."

*Troilus and Cressida* was not alone in undergoing seventeenth-century adaptation and improvement. A notable version of *King Lear* by Nahum Tate continued to be performed throughout the eighteenth century, and *Romeo and Juliet*, lightened with a happy ending, held the stage until 1845. But in these two instances the "improved" version was gradually driven off the stage by the authentic one. Not so with *Troilus and Cressida*. After Dryden's play ceased to be performed, Shakespeare's failed to take its place. Early in the nineteenth century, John Philip Kemble planned a revival and made a tentative casting, but proceeded no further. The century all but came to a close before *Troilus and Cressida* returned to the boards, and then in German.

Yet though it remained unacted, the play grew in estimation throughout the years, despite the puzzlement with which it was regarded. Readers and critics might well agree with Coleridge that "indeed, there is none of Shakespeare's plays harder to characterize." Its elusive quality, reflected in its confused classification in the sixteenth century, continued to unsettle commentators, and in 1849 Gervinus could still write that "the warmest admirers of Shakespeare are undecided about it." But what exactly were they undecided about? For one thing, the emphatic element in the play. Did it lie with the love story of Troilus and Cressida or with the intrigue among the Greeks? Coleridge thought the latter and felt that Shakespeare had "taken little pains to connect" the two parts. Samuel Johnson, quite the contrary, had thought the play "more correctly written than most of [his] compositions." Critics were also undecided about the characters. Hazlitt found Cressida "hit off with proverbial truth . . . amusing and instructive." For him Troilus held no interest, having no character and being "merely a common lover." Yet in Coleridge Troilus aroused a warm sympathy. The young prince was a potentially fascinating creature of passion and judgment. Such differences of interpretation, however, were not merely the reflection of differences in critical temperament. The text itself encourages such contradictory views. Troilus's vows of fidelity to Cressida hover so on the edge of fustian that the reader is equally justified in reading them as expressions of true love or of vain bombast. The meeting of Troilus and Cressida juxtaposes pathos and absurdity in a manner reminiscent of an optical puzzle. First, the eye perceives the cubes in diminishing perspective and then it perceives them in projection. Just so, response to Troilus's speeches can leap from identification with his emotions to alienation from them. As with Troilus's speeches, many other features of this play seem capable of producing such shifting impressions.

Nevertheless, despite the critical puzzlement, a note of unreserved admiration began to creep into nineteenth-century commentary, particularly into that of the Germans. In his conversation with Eckermann on Christmas day, 1825, Goethe advised his young friend to read *Troilus and Cressida* if he wished to see Shakespeare's mind unfettered, that is, ranging freely, unrestricted by the demands of the stage. The German theistic philosopher Ulrici regarded the play as Shakespeare's asseveration of Christian morality. By mid-century, an English editor could confess that he was prostrated "before the marvelous intellect which has produced" *Troilus and Cressida*. Slowly, the admiration which certain writers such as Hazlitt felt towards some of the individual characters began to be extended to the work as a whole.

Modern theatrical history of the play begins in Bavaria. Reportedly there was a performance of the play before King Ludwig II some time before 1898; but what is considered the first German production, and what can be considered the first modern production anywhere, was presented at Munich in that year. Offered under the auspices of the Munich Literary Society, this production attempted to depict the first performance of the work at the Globe playhouse, ruthlessly cutting the text and obscuring it under vignettes of London theatrical life. In the next year, the Society for Art and Science in Berlin sponsored a single performance of the play, and in 1904 Berliners again had the opportunity to witness the play when eight performances were given at the Deutsches Theater. Though none of these productions were wholeheartedly acclaimed, they did spark interest in the play. Budapest saw a production in 1900 and Vienna, in 1902.

Not until 1907, approximately three hundred years after it was last performed in London, was *Troilus and Cressida* presented in its original tongue. Nor did it fare well when presented. The *London Times* critic came away convinced that the play is "better left unacted," that the few "flashes of Shakespeare's poetry at its brightest" are better appreciated in the study. This advice was not followed, and happily so, for the tide was about to turn. In 1912, the Elizabethan Stage Society produced the play with William Poel as director. Since 1894, the Society, under Poel's guidance, had devoted its efforts to staging the works of Shakespeare and his contemporaries in a manner appropriate to the material. Utilizing a reconstructed Elizabethan stage and Renaissance costuming, Poel often succeeded in imparting a fresh comprehension to Shakespeare's purposes. With *Troilus and Cressida*, the procedure was similar. Stage, costume, and characterization were drawn from Elizabethan England rather than from archaic Greece. The actors were costumed in doublet, hose,

farthingale; the stage was a bare platform. The characters were English types: Thersites was a court clown,
Cressida was a fashionable English lady, Pandarus affected a cockney dialect. In this manner the production
demonstrated, to some critics at least, that the play
could be staged effectively.

For the next thirty five years performances of *Troilus
and Cressida*, though never numerous, were periodic.
Usually they were given under the auspices of a university or an art theater. In England there were six
productions between 1920 and 1940, one of these by
the Old Vic in 1923. In the United States the first
presentation took place in 1916 at Yale University, and
by the end of 1941, six more had been offered throughout the country. Germany continued to lead the way
with sixteen productions between 1918 and 1936. Thus,
little by little, the play was tested in the only way a
play can be adequately tested, through repeated performance.

Whether changes in theatrical taste precede or follow
changes in critical estimation is difficult to judge. Perhaps the critics perceive a shift in taste before it is
completely evident to society at large. In an especially
significant essay entitled " 'Discord in the Spheres':
The Universe of *Troilus and Cressida*" (1945), Una
Ellis-Fermor wrote that, "by repeated readings of the
play, helped greatly by seeing it upon the stage," she
was driven to the conclusion that the play was a great
achievement. Perhaps an age provokes a clarifying intelligence which exists equally in the creative as well as in
the critical mind. This intelligence causes the artist and
the critic, each in his own mode, to discover and render
visible new perceptions of life and art. Or so it seems
with *Troilus and Cressida*, for with its return to the
stage the play rose in critical appreciation.

During the period prior to World War II, the play was subjected to more detailed examination and discussion than it had ever undergone. A heightened respect obtained, yet the issues with which the critics wrestled were still similar to those which had beset the play from the very beginning. What kind of a play is *Troilus and Cressida?* How does Shakespeare wish us to feel towards such characters as Troilus, Ulysses, Cressida, Hector, Thersites, Pandarus? Is the play a disjointed assemblage of disconnected parts or does it have a dramatic unity of some as yet unperceived sort? Can the play perhaps have an intellectual strength which is not wholly expressed in dramatic terms?

What was substantially different during the first third of the twentieth century was not the nature of the questions, nor even of the answers, so much as the breaking down of the critical boundaries within which the answers had to be given. Earlier critical attempts sought to reconcile the play with the traditional genres. But the play would not fit into accepted notions of tragedy or comedy. The poet Heinrich Heine placed it in the domain of tragedy because it "breathes the melancholy spirit of Melpomene rather than the gaiety of Thalia." But he did so reluctantly. To him *Troilus and Cressida* was neither comedy nor tragedy, but "Shakespeare's most characteristic creation. We can acknowledge its great excellence only in general terms; for a detailed judgment we should need the help of that new aesthetics which has not yet been written." Since then several people have tried to write such an aesthetics for the play.

In 1931, W. W. Lawrence linked *Troilus and Cressida* with *Measure for Measure* and *All's Well that Ends Well* as members of a new type: problem comedy. The essential characteristic of such a type, he argued, is "that a perplexing and distressing complication in human life is presented in a spirit of high seriousness," though without tragic outcome. Lawrence insisted on the special quality of these plays, specifically distinguishing *Troilus and Cressida* from tragicomedy and satire. At first this new designation of "Shakespeare's problem plays," derived from the post-Ibsen type of realistic drama, seemed to offer a vantage point for understanding the disparate elements of the text. Several critics, notably E. M. W. Tillyard, adopted the term. But later critics found the definition inadequate. Perhaps it suggests too systematic an approach to serious issues, a discursive approach unsuited to the terrible discord and frivolous irrationality so evident in the play.

Some years later O. J. Campbell argued that *Triolus and Cressida* was not, indeed, a problem play but a comical satire. Sophisticated in tone, devastating in attack, the play, according to him, mocked the foolish and decadent posturings of Troilus. But the interpretation of *Troilus and Cressida* as a comical satire has also proved unsatisfactory because the objects proposed as the targets of Shakespeare's satire have lacked either universality or consistency. As a satire against practiced lust or foolish love-making, the play is clearly fragmentary and insubstantial. As a satire against war, it is haphazard. But most important, as a satire on any subject, it does not possess one essential ingredient: moral rectitude. Inherent in a satiric attitude, whether that of Aristophanes, Jonson, or Marston, is conviction of moral superiority. The satirist is devastating because he possesses the true vision which others, whose images are reflected in the written work, do not have. Like Jonson, the satirist administers purges to his contemporaries in order to restore them to moral and social health. The structure of his work is predicated on a concept of purified—one might almost say puritanic—behavior, even though the concept is merely founded upon the personal standards of the writer, and the denouement is a vindication of that concept. Men are brought to accept admonishment or to envision the true way.

If such is satire, *Troilus and Cressida* is not satire. Satirical elements there may be. The treatment of Ajax and Achilles has been so regarded. But Shakespeare is too detached; the drama lacks a consistent moral tone, a point of faith or attitude against which the behavior of the characters can be measured. The denouement vindicates no moral view. The Greeks conquer, but basely and by chance. The Trojans are defeated, but do not fall gallantly. Hector's final victory is won over a golden shell of armor. The world that remains is a world of appetite in which one can devour or be devoured.

Less clear-cut but almost as long-lived as the dispute over genre has been disagreement about the major figures. Coleridge could take for granted the portrait of Cressida enunciated by Ulysses. To him she is a creature of "wanton spirits." Troilus, by contrast, is capable of "profound affection." Increasingly these simple assumptions have been challenged, much more so with recent efforts to define the play's nature in fresh terms. Not so much that new critical views of the characters have appeared, as that opposing views have become more extreme. To one Shakespearean scholar, L. L. Schücking, Troilus is "an ideal figure." To another, O. J. Campbell, he is an object of satire, "an Italianate English roué." He and Cressida are viewed as "two virtuosi in sensuality" whose actions were meant to draw a critical and derisive response from the audience. They are to be rejected, he as well as she. More recently, differences of interpretation have continued to grow,

and although the majority of critics tend to regard
Troilus with Schücking's rather than with Campbell's
eyes, there are points to be scored for both sides.

Not until after World War II, however, did the play
come fully into its own. Since 1945 it has been produced at all the major Shakespearean festivals, twice at
Stratford-upon-Avon in England. Between 1951 and
1955, three different translations of the play were produced in West Germany. In 1959 the Holland Festival
production was sent to Paris to represent the Dutch
theater at the Théâtre des Nations. On both sides of
the Atlantic, the play has been presented in modern-
dress versions. Tyrone Guthrie's Old Vic production of
1956 set the action in a nineteenth century sort of
Ruritania, and Jack Landau's Stratford, Connecticut,
production of 1961 set it during the American Civil
War. Both versions sought to throw the futility of war
into relief against settings more familiar and more immediate for the larger audiences being reached in the
post-war era. Whatever the merits of such treatments,
they are reflections of the widespread recognition that
*Troilus and Cressida* is, in the words of the Polish critic
Jan Kott, "amazing and modern."

The modernity of the play was apparent to Bernard
Shaw who observed that with *Troilus and Cressida*
Shakespeare was ready to begin the twentieth century.
At the very end of World War II, Ellis-Fermor stressed
the close connection between the image of the play and
the reality of contemporary life. She asserted that the
post-war world was capable of discerning something new
in *Troilus and Cressida* because:

> our actual experience of disintegration and disrup-
> tion, so unlike that of any age between [Shakespeare's
> and our own], has thrown fresh light upon the nature

and foundations of what we call civilization; prospects once mercifully rare are now common and familiar, and much that has not, in the interval, been generally forced upon the imagination, now lies upon the common road for every man's necessary consideration.

Implied in this view is the concept that in the mirrored image of the play was prefigured "the downfall of the principles of order and value in the world of man's creation." Though she does not state so explicitly, Miss Ellis-Fermor was actually describing the existential drama, a Sartrian "assertion of chaos as the ultimate fact of being." Seen from this point of view, she argues, *Troilus and Cressida* must be judged a major dramatic triumph, for "the idea of chaos . . . has by a supreme act of artistic mastery been given form."

The very distaste aroused in earlier readers by the unsavory love affair and the ludicrous war fitted well the temperament of the Atomic Age. Thersites's refrain of "war and lechery" confirms the modern sense of alienation. The conclusions that he draws from the postures of the Greeks and Trojans are those that we are too ready to accept: honor is vainglory, truth is simplicity, faith is fashion, reason is rhetoric, and love, fair love, is nothing but lechery. For a present-day society that has quite thoroughly exiled all but the fantasy hero, debunking the antique heroes of archaic Greece is merest farce, and, more than that, a disenchanted look at existence.

Such a philosophical climate does not make tragedy possible, and, in fact, the work of tragedy, that is, the facing of values and of death, has passed over to comedy, not the comedy of lightness, but of darkness. Miss Ellis-Fermor, though excluding *Troilus and Cressida* from the catalogue of tragedy, did not attempt to define its nature. However, Jan Kott in *Shakespeare Our Con-temporary* and Robert Kimbrough in an extended study of the play, beholding the work from substantially the same vantage point as she, have seen it as an expression of the same spirit which informs contemporary "dark" or "grotesque" comedy.

Such comedy is essentially realistic and amoral, yet at the same time supremely humanistic. The archetypal action is man's confrontation with nothingness. Man's ideas having been found wanting, man's existence alone remains an existence highly personal, incapable of being attached to attitudes or groups. At this level of existence, honor is vestigial, love is sensation, philoso-phy is mere advantage. Others are self-interested, and even a man like Thersites who condemns mankind does so not in way of truth but in way of pleasure. Since, in this comic universe, there is no god, the people cry out to themselves for answers to quintessential questions. What prevents such work from being tragic is the ab-sence of worthiness and the presence of the ludicrous. There is nothing worth dying for, and so living itself is grotesque. In tragedy, Kott notes, "death confirms the existence of the absolute." Where there is no abso-lute value, death is circumstantial and an absurd folly prevails.

Today *Troilus and Cressida* has assumed the status of a major work. Seen as an "image of chaos" or as an image of a grotesque world where "love is poisoned from the outset," the very features of the play which formerly were regarded as faulty have now come to be seen as strengths. For the stage director *Troilus and Cressida* is virtually a new work. It is not burdened by a longstanding theatrical or critical tradition. It has features which speak directly to a contemporary audi-ence. Though the story is ancient, the atmosphere is modern, and that is a decided advantage for a director. As a result, he has both an artistic and psychological freedom in dealing with the text. Yet the history of the play must put him on guard. No other play of Shakespeare's has undergone such an extreme shift of favor. No other play has defied definition so determinedly. Not that its scenes, individually, have been so puzzling, but efforts to define the play's total impression have resulted in unusually divergent conclusions. Every director of Shakespeare faces two crucial challenges. The first stems from the philosophical character of many of the scenes. He must find ways of giving the discussions on value, order, will, and appetite theatrical expressiveness in an age of lazy and untuned ears. The second arises from the contradictory ways in which the principal figures may be regarded. He must coax from the text a comprehensive insight into the play, rich enough to bind together all the views of the characters. The insights of Ellis-Fermor and Kott are valuable and suggestive, but they are not easily given theatrical form. The attempt to create a distinctive context finds its clearest representative in modern-dress productions. In his Old Vic production, Sir Tyrone Guthrie sought to create an atmosphere of Trojan decadence through an *opera buffo* caricature of *fin de siècle* militarism with Cressida and Pandarus inhabitants of a Viennese-styled demimonde and Thersites a scabrous foreign correspondent.

This method, however, is not the only way, nor necessarily the preferred way, to achieve unity of impression or immediacy of effect. In the New York Shakespeare Festival production, Joseph Papp chose to remain within the accepted framework of ancient Greece and Troy. Principally through working with the actors rather than by imposing a directorial frame, he

The Festival Shakespeare *Troilus and Cressida* explored the relationships between the characters. As his directorial statement illustrates, he saw in the victimization of Cressida the key to the text. The peculiar history of the play makes his directorial statement significant, for we are still discovering the possibilities of this astonishing play.

# Directing *Troilus and Cressida*

### ◄§ *by Joseph Papp*

Every director, despite his need for objectivity, finds he has certain prejudices about the characters in a play. Complete neutrality is not possible, nor is it desirable. Confronted with a text teeming with living creatures who possess complex psychological make-ups, the director must have the ability to assess the characters within their own milieu and then subject them to modern scrutiny. The prevailing moods and attitudes of our times as well as the nature, taste, and outlook of actor and director shape the conception of the play and the roles within it. Another word, then, for prejudice might be "slant," or better yet, "interpretation"—a point of view.

In *Troilus and Cressida* it is almost possible to dislike every character in the play, for in it we find that we can choose from the most despicable assortment of low-life ever crammed together in a single work: panders, traitors, connivers, whores, cuckolds, seducers, rapists, lechers, murderers, liars, fornicators, and adulterers. And yet in no other play of Shakespeare's do we hear the words "honor" and "truth" as often as we do in *Troilus and Cressida*.

It is this contradiction that compelled me in rehearsal to single out the sometime-hero of the play, Troilus, as the greatest offender against decency. My feelings were that he was a cad and Cressida, his victim. Try as I might I couldn't bring myself to feel any sympathy for Troilus's caterwauling and protestations of immaculate love. I felt he applied a double standard in honor, and to me this was immoral.

I blamed him for Cressida's plight more than I did Pandarus or the Valentino of the Greeks, Diomedes. This attitude was so strong that it created an unfortunate conflict between me and the actor playing the role of Troilus. Even more unfortunately, it worked against some of the sympathy that the playwright had for Troilus. Shakespeare showed greater tolerance for human failings than I did.

The crucial point in the Troilus-Cressida relationship is reached in Act IV, Scene iv. Here Troilus is confronted with a decision, the outcome of which, in my estimation, shows what kind of a man he really is and paves the way for Cressida's "unfaithfulness." But to understand the significance of this moment, it is necessary to begin with our first meeting with Troilus.

Here we encounter a young man in the throes of adolescent love (I. i.). There is more than a touch of Romeo in Troilus's lamentations, not the Romeo in love with Juliet, but the earlier Romeo rejected by Rosaline. Troilus throws his armor to the floor protesting his inability to fight the Greeks while his heart is breaking with unrequited love for Cressida.

Anyone who has loved knows the pain of it, and the audience should identify with Troilus. However, the presence of Pandarus uttering his *double-entendres* muddies the pure waters of Troilus's woe. It is not an accident but a deliberate choice on the part of the playwright to place the "dirty old man" and the young anguished lover together in the scene. Something of Pandarus inevitably rubs off on Troilus, though the perception of this corrupting influence may not be readily apparent to the audience so early in the play.

The most interesting piece of information about Troilus supplied by this opening encounter is his attitude toward the war:

> Peace, you ungracious clamors! Peace, rude sounds!
> Fools on both sides! Helen must needs be fair,
> When with your blood you daily paint her thus.
> I cannot fight upon this argument;
> It is too starved a subject for my sword.
>
> (93–97)

He is soon to eat these words and thus baits the trap in which he will be caught.

To Cressida, the war is remote (I. ii.). It has little meaning for her except that men are involved in the fighting. Pandarus has been pressing her hard to yield to a tryst with Troilus. Though she is not opposed to the idea, evidently she has deep reservations. Her toying with Pandarus is a device to ward off the conclusion for which he is pressing. She achieves this by disparaging the praise that Pandarus heaps on Troilus. There is little doubt that she is stimulated, or rather, titillated by the prospect of the affair, but is not quite ready for the act.

It is too simple an analysis to interpret Cressida's preoccupation with sexual allusions as definite proof of sluttishness. Her banter and flirtatiousness appear to be defensive in nature rather than overt manifestations of raging sexual desire. In our times we know that there are many who speak freely about sex and yet do not match their actions to their words, and conversely, there are those who say little and do much. Therefore, we cannot assume that Cressida's ready tongue expresses her past behavior. Clearly Pandarus has been endeavoring to overcome a reluctance in her.

There is no doubt, despite her seeming indifference, that Cressida's heart is beating very fast as she awaits the appearance of Troilus. Her sexual references become more pointed as she begins to consider yielding to him. The first of these is in a punning remark that curiously parallels Pandarus's references to the process of baking in his scene with Troilus (I. i. 14–28). In this early scene Pandarus warns the young prince that matters of the heart take time and compares wooing with the preparation needed to bake cake. He refers to the grinding, the bolting, the kneading, the heating of the oven, and so on. In speaking to Cressida, Pandarus enumerates Troilus's virtues, and chides her for lacking appreciation of them. He calls them "the spice and salt that season a man." Cressida responds with: "Ay, a minced man; and then to be baked with no date in the pie, for then the man's date is out." (265–269) Within the context of events and characters, the obscenity underlying the comments is obvious.

In Cressida's next speech the sexual content is made quite explicit. She warns Pandarus that he must bear the responsibility for the outcome of her rendezvous with Troilus.

> *Pandarus.* You are such a woman a man knows not at what ward you lie.
> *Cressida.* Upon my back to defend my belly. . . .

And then after a pun on the words watch and ward, she says:

> If I cannot ward what I would not have hit, I can watch you for telling how I took the blow; unless it swell past hiding, and then it's past watching.
> *Pandarus.* You are such another!

> (270–283)

The actor playing Pandarus argued that Cressida was undoubtedly a light and loose woman who had experienced previous sexual relations with men. He used the external evidence of her sex banter to press his point. I took exception to this view, first because there was nothing in the text to corroborate the fact, but, more importantly, because I felt it was necessary to separate what people said from what they did. And, in fact, what Cressida said was contradictory. Her words are strongly indicative of her chastity, of her fear of becoming pregnant, of her fear that "Things won are done." She says in a revealing soliloquy (addressed to women, I think) that "Men prize the thing ungained. . . ." She admits her great love for Troilus but "Yet hold I off." This is not the expression of a tease, but of a woman with realistic recognition that men are hot in the pursuit and cool when they attain the prize. She is unrealistic when she imagines that endless wooing can be a way of love. The sweetness she feels as a result of Troilus's desire for her is a condition that cannot be maintained indefinitely. In this respect, she is girlish and immature.

In her speech there is also evidence of her fear of domination by men: "Achievement is command; ungained, beseech." This quality reveals itself later in her affair with Diomedes. But to any feeling soul she is here more to be pitied than censured.

In the final analysis her fears are unfortunately corroborated. Ironically, this mixture of fear and wanting and reservation encourages the very result that she would avoid.

This scene (II. ii.) has many ramifications, not the least of which is the introduction of Hector and the rest of Priam's family. But we are mainly interested in Troilus's behavior here and its effect on his relationship with Cressida.

The conflict of the scene stems from an offer by the Greeks to conclude hostilities if Helen is returned. Hector says "Let Helen go." To him she is not worth the deaths of so many thousands of men. Troilus, in heated blood, denounces his older brother. He talks fiercely of honor and manhood. He attacks his brother Helenus who speaks of reason. Troilus cries out to him: "You fur your gloves with reason. . . . Reason and respect/Make livers pale and lustihood deject." (37–50)

Trying to prove his point in regard to "honor" and commitment, Troilus embarks upon a rhetorical explanation of honor. He uses the example of his taking a wife, and says:

> How may I avoid,
> Although my will distaste what it elected,
> The wife I chose? There can be no evasion
> To blench from this and to stand firm by *honor*.[1]
>
> (65–68)

Then we hear Troilus advocate, as a point of honor, the principle of a man's commitment to a woman once a promise is made—words that, had Cressida overheard them, would have allayed the anxieties she expressed in Act I, Scene ii: "Things won are done." He says:

> We turn not back the silks upon the merchant
> When we have soiled them, nor the remainder viands
> We do not throw in unrespective sieve
> Because we now are full.
>
> (69–72)

He probably does not remember his previous lines about Helen:

---

[1] Italics in the speeches cited are inserted by the author.

Fools on both sides! Helen must needs be fair,
When with your blood you daily paint her thus.
I cannot fight upon this argument;
It is too starved a subject for my sword.

(I. i. 94–97)

Now he calls Helen "a pearl/Whose price hath launched above a thousand ships. . . ." (81–82) "she is a theme of honor and renown." (199) Troilus now feels the war is glorious. Honor is the subject of his story.

This scene I would characterize as a "set-up scene" because the character who violently defends a course of action in the name of "honor" will soon face a situation where his honor will be put to the test—not in the glorious terms of war, but in the personal terms of love. That he will fail the test is the crux of my argument.

Pandarus's visit with Helen and Paris (III. i.) has an indirect but significant effect on the scene that follows—the meeting of Troilus and Cressida. Pandarus's ostensible purpose is to secure Paris's aid in covering Troilus's absence from the palace. Here once more Shakespeare displays his extraordinary technique of "infection by association." He will employ Pandarus as a "carrier" who will both infect and be infected. He will have him flit around the royal boudoir, a swamp saturated with stale perfume, its inhabitants a pair of loveless lovers breathing the tired, dank air of oversated sexuality. And he will sit on a silken bed and immerse himself in the rank sweat of a bawdy song, and then he is ready to carry the germs which cling to him into the next scene of unstained love. He says in parting:

> Is this the generation of love—hot blood, hot thoughts, and hot deeds? Why, they are vipers. Is love a generation of vipers? (130–132)

Although he seems to be expressing disapproval of lust, Pandarus would in truth have it no other way.

Going directly and breathlessly to Troilus (III. ii.), he asks, "Have you seen my cousin?" Troilus's reply, steeped as it is in death imagery, is a revelation of the nature of Troilus's character and feelings. It contains none of the buoyant, life-loving lines of Romeo. Shakespeare here shows us that things are dark and murky. The lines show Troilus's preoccupation with himself. It reveals his striving for an ideal of sorts in the context of a corrupt environment. The lines possess all the outer qualities of young love awaiting a most delicious encounter. But the taint that will soon stain this love affair is already in evidence. It has been carried over from the previous scene; it is a product of a "cormorant" war with an absurd cause.

Troilus stalks about Cressida's door "Like a strange soul upon the Stygian banks." (III. ii. 7ff.) He asks Pandarus to be his "Charon," the grim ferryman of the dead. He wants to "wallow in the lily beds," *wallow*, an unlovely word for a lover. When he says: "O gentle Pandar, From Cupid's shoulder *pluck his painted wings*," I shudder at the picture. Pandarus leaves to fetch his ward and Troilus goes on in his death "ecstasy." Back and forth goes the panting and expectant Pandarus, infecting the stage with his contagion.

I am trying not to be carried away by my prejudices, and hope that they are founded in the truth of the play. While it is not difficult in Shakespeare to extract a particular line or group of lines to prove a point, it is equally easy to quote a line proving the opposite. The most dependable gauge lies in feeling the total effect of the work.

Troilus's speeches just discussed have a specific texture produced not only by the choice of words, but also by their sounds and their construction. Even if we were to extract these speeches from the rest of the play we could not escape the sickness in them. It is not that lovers so deeply in love do not talk about dying. Shakespeare makes it very clear in all of the plays preceding *Troilus and Cressida* what he considers to be true love: it is simply that true lovers care more for one another than they do for themselves. The final act of true love is demonstrated for all times in *Romeo and Juliet*: "O churl! Drunk all, and left no friendly drop/To help me after?" (*Romeo and Juliet* V. iii. 163–164)

I cannot believe that Troilus is capable of love, not because of his youth, but because of a defect in character. He has a distorted view of the relationship of man and woman. If I sympathize with him at all, it is as one sympathizes with those who are victims of feelings and events they fail to comprehend. If there is a "villain" in the piece, it is Ulysses. He operates from a highly conscious level. He has the talent to manipulate because he is capable of removing himself and looking on. Troilus is not. Troilus is impulsive, rash, and a prisoner of uncontrollable feelings. One may prefer his inconsistency to Ulysses' clear-cut consistency, but, as the director, I must hold the view that each character is responsible for his acts and I must do what is difficult to do in real life: pass moral judgments. But I can only do this within the terms set forth by the playwright.

Troilus's speeches before the entrance of Cressida smack of something unwholesome. They sound false to my ears. They jar my esthetic. This is so even though I recognize that Troilus is not aware of any shortcomings in his love, and also that his feelings, such as they are, are genuinely painful. He is not feigning anything. The experience is real; Troilus is not a conscious hypocrite. Nevertheless, he is driven by inner forces that he fails to understand. From the spectator's point of view it is not necessary to analyze these forces, for we see them working.

Shakespeare, the master of the English language, reveals character mainly through speech. A single tone or stroke can be extremely revealing. One minor note, barely heard, but very much present, tells the listener that Troilus's speech of great love is not authentic. One deft touch, a subtle rearrangement of words and images, tells us the difference between Romeo's puppy love for Rosaline and his profound love for Juliet.

The ear is the key to it. We eventually condition our ear to the sounds of William Shakespeare, and when we do, we learn to understand his way of communicating. As our sensitivities to him increase, we begin to manage the more complex sounds, the counterpoint of a scene. How attunement to a single word can affect an entire role was revealed in my work with the actor playing the role of Troilus. Throughout rehearsals, he resisted any disparaging aspects of Troilus's character. Then we came to a crucial speech in Act III, Scene ii, one already mentioned. Troilus, anticipating the ecstasy with Cressida, imagines himself about to "wallow in the lily beds" (11). When I brought this figure of speech to his attention, the actor conceded that it suggested to him the image of a pig and that Troilus's choice of words did indicate some distortion in the character's make-up and feelings. Although I won the point, I felt I had erred in pressing it. I did not want to turn him against the character, since every actor must justify the actions of the character he portrays, no matter how distasteful they may be. Balancing the actor's objective evaluation of the person he is playing with his subjective involvement in the part is a delicate matter. The result of the foregoing exchange upset the balance, and pushed the

actor into playing the "villain." It took many days of
rehearsal to restore the balance. If I were to do it again,
I would approach the problem more obliquely, and
attempt to obtain the necessary result without a direct
attack upon the character.

We come now to the encounter—the first meeting of
Troilus and Cressida (III. ii.). Entwined with the lovers
is the master of the grand design, Pandarus, the pimp,
urging his charge and his fair-haired boy to "rub on."
"Words pay no debts," he admonishes Troilus, "give
her deeds." He presses them together. They kiss. A long
kiss. When they come up for air, he presses them
together again with "Nay, you shall fight your hearts
out ere I part you." (49–52)

The modern audience seems not to recognize the "im-
morality" of the situation. It finds the situation funny.
Undoubtedly there is a kind of humor in it, but if this
were a contemporary play about a parentless young girl,
with a neurotic fear of sex, being pushed into bed by
her neurotic guardian with a nice, wealthy, neurotic
young man, the reaction might be somewhat different.
The audience might still find the circumstances amusing, but only if the whole play were an obvious comedy.
But in *Troilus and Cressida* the overtones prevent a
lighthearted reaction. The laughs, when they come, are
dark and dirty.

Let us consider the entire "movement," which starts
here and ends with the forced parting of the "lovers."

Pandarus, all afire, leaves them alone for a moment,
to make ready the bedroom. We are surprised at
Cressida's line at this moment and Troilus's answer.
She says: "Will you walk in, my lord?" She, Cressida,
the girl who has told us that she will hold off, makes the
first approach. And Troilus, he who is so hot, whom we

would expect to lift her into his arms and carry her
straight to bed, ignores the invitation and instead says:
"O Cressid, how often have I wished me thus!" (61–
62) An evasive answer to a direct question.

What is going on here? Have the characters been
reversed? Is Cressida anxious for bed and Troilus appre-
hensive? There is no doubt that Troilus stops her, and
Cressida, not wanting to be thought too forward or, perhaps, having her own doubts about him, does not press
her request further. Instead she joins him in the delay-
ing game. His turn-about has evidently embarrassed her,
and she stumblingly grasps his unwelcome bait with
"Wished, my lord? . . ." Her next lines, "The gods
grant—O my lord!" (63–64), emanate from the dis-
maying fact that his hesitation has placed the burden
of the initiative on her shoulders; thus, she consciously
reverts to the role of a helpless little girl fearful of the
consequences—the accepted role of a woman in the
man-woman relationship. Had Troilus behaved like a
man and accepted her invitation this would not have
been necessary.

There is no doubt that Cressida has real fears in
submitting to Troilus. She voiced them earlier. It is
highly possible, therefore, that the preceding lines are
grounded in these fears. But they are highly ambivalent.
Her instinct tells her that Troilus prefers her in the
romanticized version. As soon as she acts the helpless
female, Troilus springs to life. She has given him the
means of playing the lover.

Troilus's feelings are also ambivalent. He is ready to
heap high-sounding phrases on her head, but the fact
that the situation itself, an assignation arranged by a
third and dubious party, is lacking in pure romance,
to say the least, makes him uncomfortable. He wishes
Cressida to be one hundred per cent pure. But this is

already impossible because of the nature of the arrangement. Therefore, he requires more romancing before
he can accept Cressida in bed. "Assurances" may be a
better word. Cressida is highly conscious of the same
thing. She would have been happy to get on with it,
burying her fears in Troilus's arms. But the lad put a
damper on the proceedings.

The exchange that follows is a masterpiece of decep-
tion. On the surface we see a hesitant Cressida seeking
guarantees that Troilus will be true. Unlike Juliet, she
is not discussing marriage. She is preoccupied with performance. Men she calls monsters because they "swear
more performance than they are able, and yet reserve
an ability that they never perform, vowing more than
the perfection of ten and discharging less than the tenth
part of one. They that have the voice of lions and the
act of hares. . . ." (86–91) There is no doubt that this
taunting of Troilus's sexual prowess was provoked by
his previous remark: "This is the monstruosity in love,
lady, that the will is infinite and *the execution confined*;
that the desire is boundless and the act *a slave to limit*."
(82–85) Cressida senses that he is copping a plea and
pressures him to defend his manhood. In the same vein,
he continues with: "Praise us as we are tasted, allow us
as we prove; our head shall go bare till merit crown it."
(92–94) He has finally assured her that he will be good
in bed. Somewhat fearful of his commitment, he begins
to poeticize it with extravagant claims of his truth and
undying love: "Troilus shall be such to Cressid, as what
envy can say worst shall be a mock for his *truth*, and
what *truth* can speak *truest* not *truer* than Troilus."
(98–100)

The few lines of Troilus's at the beginning reveal the
nature of the scene. He asks, "What too *curious dreg*

espies my sweet lady in the fountain of our love?"
(66–67) The exchange that follows answers this question. It is not a love scene, not Romeo and Juliet in
content, though it appears to be so in form. The contrast between this meeting and the meeting of the star-
crossed lovers is overwhelmingly apparent. Troilus feels
he has gotten Cressida too easily, and so he distrusts her
from the start. Now that she has surrendered, he feels
this distrust; yet that very morning he thought her
cruel for holding out so long. He keeps saying in effect,
"Why can't you be like me?" She was more enticing as
an abstraction than a reality. Not that she is less beautiful in the flesh, more so perhaps, but Troilus has a hard
time dealing with the real thing. This is the hypocrisy
unconsciously working in him. He wants her to give
herself to him, but if she does, she becomes a whore.
There is no equivalent designation for the male in the
situation. Cressida is much more honest and realistic.
She accepts the circumstances for what they are, and
although she has the greater risk (pregnancy), she is
less demanding. She doesn't ask for undying faith; she
wants him to love her now. Troilus is more concerned
about his chastity than she is about hers.

In contrast, Juliet sings the sweet music of true love
in one of the most lyrical speeches in all of Shakespeare.
Note the difference.

> Thou knowest the mask of night is on my face;
> Else would a maiden blush bepaint my cheek
> For that which thou hast heard me speak to-night.
> Fain would I dwell on form—fain, fain deny
> What I have spoke; but farewell compliment!
> Dost thou love me? I know thou wilt say 'Ay';
> And I will take thy word. Yet, if thou swear'st,
> Thou mayst prove false. At lovers' perjuries,

They say Jove laughs. O gentle Romeo,
If thou dost love, pronounce it faithfully.
Or if thou thinkest I am too quickly won,
I'll frown, and be perverse, and say thee nay,
So thou wilt woo; but else, not for the world.
In truth, fair Montague, I am too fond,
And therefore thou mayst think my 'havior light;
But trust me, gentleman, I'll prove more true
Than those that have more cunning to be strange.
I should have been more strange, I must confess,
But that thou overheard'st ere I was ware,
My true-love passion. Therefore pardon me,
And not impute this yielding to light love,
Which the dark night hath so discovered.

(*Romeo and Juliet*, II. ii.)

Romeo begins to swear by the moon to show his faith, but she chides him for that. The moon is changeable. "What shall I swear by?" he asks. And Juliet replies: "Do not swear at all; Or if thou wilt, swear by thy gracious self, Which is the god of my idolatry, And I'll believe thee." And then, in one of the deepest expressions of feminine love, Juliet says these lines:

My bounty is as boundless as the sea,
My love as deep; the more I give to thee,
The more I have, for both are infinite.

There is no fear in Juliet. Her deep love gives her a strength and certainty that make it possible for her to take her own life without hesitation. But she draws this strength from her beloved Romeo. It is a two-way street, both give and take from one another, an exchange that makes them invincible.

The reader may get the impression that I am unhappy that Troilus and Cressida are not Romeo and Juliet.

This is not the case at all. The difference merely serves
to illuminate the point I have tried to make in the Central Park production; namely, that Cressida's downfall,
if you will, is given impetus by Troilus's inability to
love. Cressida, in spite of her character, is the more
capable of love, as will be demonstrated.

We return to Troilus, who has worked himself into
a passion of words, vowing his unalterable "truth."
Cressida obviously assumes he must be ready now, for
she asks once again: "Will you walk in, my lord?" (101)
Pandarus's entrance at this point and his words: "What,
blushing still? Have you not done talking yet?" indicate
that Troilus did not respond to the twice-given invitation. Cressida, evidently impatient, decides to bring
matters to a conclusion with, "Well, uncle, what folly
I commit, I dedicate to you." (104–105 ff.) Pandarus,
also impatient, gets right down to the subject at hand
with: "If my lord get a boy of you, you'll give him me."
The next line, although directed at Cressida, must
certainly worry Troilus. "Be true to my lord," says
Pandarus, "*if he flinch,* chide me for it." Performance
again being put to the test. "True" means good performance. Troilus offers two highly dubious assurances:
"You know now your hostages: your uncle's word and
my firm faith." Here again, a comment on performance.
But Troilus still makes no move to go in. Cressida
bursts out with "Boldness comes to me now and brings
me heart./Prince Troilus, I have loved you night and
day/For many weary months." But this is not good
enough for the Prince. He has to ask, "Why was my
Cressid then so hard to win?" (118)

Now Cressida twists and turns. Her words pour out
in a torrent of truths, half-truths, threats to leave. "Stop
my mouth," she cries, putting her lips close to his,
which he cannot escape if he did wish it. It is a curious

mixture of wiles and real feeling, ending with an accusa-
tion that Troilus cannot let go by unchallenged, that
he "loves not." (135–157) This launches him into a
rhapsodic aria of ideal love—an ideal woman to match
him—the ideal lover. He talks of constancy, integrity,
winnowed purity, and *truth*, reiterated four times.
Cressida sees that he is aroused and matches him with
"In that I'll war with you." But Troilus has only begun.
Now he eulogizes:

> True swains in love shall in the world to come
> Approve their *truth* by Troilus. When their rhymes,
> Full of protest, of oath and big compare,
> Wants similes, *truth tired with iteration*,
> "As *true* as steel, . . . as turtle to her mate" . . .
> Yet, after all comparisons of *truth*,
> As *truth*'s authentic author to be cited,
> "As *true* as Troilus" shall crown up the verse
> And sanctify the numbers.
>
> (174–184)

The moment is approaching. Cressida launches into a
great vow of fidelity (which might have been avoided if
Troilus had not been so reluctant). Whereas Troilus's
key word throughout has been "truth," Shakespeare, the
mischief-maker, gives Cressida the word "false" to play
with. "If I be false or swerve a hair from truth," she
begins. And after drawing a number of similes equal
to Troilus's, she concludes, "Yea [a singing word], let
them say, to stick the heart of falsehood,/'As false as
Cressid.'"

Now ensues an unholy "wedding" ceremony, with
Pandarus, the high priest, performing the ritual. At the
conclusion, all the parties say "Amen," and the principals rush offstage to consummate the "marriage" with
Pandarus's blessing ringing in their ears:

I will show you a chamber which bed, because it
shall not speak of your pretty encounters, press
it to death.

In ecstatic triumph, he ends with the couplet:

And Cupid grant all tongue-tied maidens here
Bed, chamber, Pandar to provide this gear!
(209–213)

In the Delacorte Theater production, the first intermission took place at this point. As with any point
selected for the interval of a Shakespearean play, we
lose something. For the very next scene (III. iii.) opens
with a speech by Cressida's father, who had deserted
to the Greeks, asking the Greek council to exchange an
important Trojan prisoner for his daughter. The juxta-
position of this request and the ending of the previous
scene was obviously intended by the playwright. The
plot is further complicated by the introduction of Diomedes, the man sent to fetch Cressida, and with whom
she will soon break the oath made to Troilus. There is
more than the obvious meaning in Diomedes' acceptance of his assignment: "This shall I undertake, and
'tis a *burden* Which I am proud to *bear*." (III. iii.
36–37)
Shakespeare has no hesitation in piling irony upon
irony when he has the wanton Paris meet Diomedes in
the business of the prisoner exchange (IV. i.). Paris
feels guilty about his mission and admits as much when
he sends Aeneas ahead to tell Troilus the bitter news.
(35–49) "Rouse him," he instructs Aeneas, "and give
him note of our approach. . . ./I fear we shall be much
unwelcome." Aeneas's reply might imply criticism of
Paris: "That I assure you./Troilus had rather Troy were
borne to Greece/Than Cressid borne from Troy."

Paris's answer again shows his guilt. "There is no help./ The bitter disposition of the time/Will have it so."

Paris, eager to have Aeneas bear the brunt of the news, stalls for time, and engages Diomedes in what starts out as light conversation. He is unprepared for the bitter flow of invective that Diomedes heaps on Helen and on the absurdity of the war. There is much to be commended in Diomedes' speech. Apart from Hector's rational condemnation of the war over Helen no character in the play makes as much sense. Yet Diomedes' hatred for Helen and the suffering war she has caused must have some effect on his attitude toward all women, especially Cressida. The impression we get is that Diomedes looks upon all women as whores, who are to be treated accordingly.

The sounds of Paris's and Diomedes' voices have barely died away in the early-morning stillness of the streets when Troilus and Cressida appear (IV. ii.). Troilus is in the lead, making for the gate, while his partner seems anxious to keep him longer. All appears to be perfectly reasonable. The man has had his fill, a normal biological reaction. He is sated, surfeited in fact, and wants to depart. We might conceivably construe his first words to Cressida as a manifestation of concern for her health. "Dear, trouble not yourself; the morn is cold." She clings to him, winding her arms about his neck, and he gently removes them and begins to lead her back to the bedroom with this gentle admonishment: "To bed, to bed. Sleep kill those pretty eyes,/And give as soft attachment to thy senses/As infants' empty of all thought!" Here again his choice of images gives us insight into his feelings: "*kill* those pretty eyes," "infants' *empty* of all thought." Troilus still speaks in the poetic vein, but his heart doesn't seem to be in his words. We are somewhat disappointed in the lover who, the night before, pledged his love to the death with such great eloquence. We like to believe that love does not disappear after the sexual act, but that instead it deepens and grows richer. And here we see the girl Cressida, the one who uttered all those cynical comments about love, acting very much the smitten one. Her voice is soft and pleading. She senses his rejection of her and turns away from him with "Good morrow then." All this makes Troilus terribly uncomfortable and somewhat irritable. He speaks more insistently, "I prithee now, to bed." She turns back to him and asks plaintively, "Are you aweary of me?" Troilus protests too much:

O Cressida! But that the busy day,
Waked by the lark, hath roused the ribald crows,
And dreaming night will hide our joys no longer,
I would not from thee.

(8–11)

His response tells us that he *is* "aweary" of her. And Cressida knows this too. Her initial fears are being borne out before her. "Things won are done. . . . Men prize the thing ungained." These were the maxims that led her to say "Yet hold I off." But the poor girl succumbed to the pressure of her uncle and her love for Troilus. And here she stands in the cold morning light, shivering and fallen. We can barely hear her say, "Night hath been too brief," as she makes one more try for Troilus's tenderness. His irritation and his being forced into making a difficult adjustment prompts his attack on "night," the first phrase of which could be interpreted as applying to Cressida: "Beshrew the witch!" But he continues in the same cruel phraseology that has become familiar to us—harsh and ugly sounding words—anti-love in character. Listen: . . . "With venomous wights she stays/As tediously as hell, but flies the grasps of love/With wings more momentary-swift than thought." And at the end of this soaring eloquence, he says in the vernacular, "You will catch cold and curse me." (12–15) What a fall from the heights is this! Worse yet, his concern for her health has undergone a change. Now he is worried that she will blame *him* if she catches cold. The intrusion of the mundane into a great love affair reminds me of the old joke: "My darling, for your love I will climb Mount Everest, cross the Sahara, walk through fire, swim the Atlantic and if it is not drizzling tonight, I'll come to see you."

Troilus, seeing that his words are getting him nowhere, starts to make for the gate again. Cressida, no pride left, tearfully pleads with him to stay: "Prithee, tarry," she cries, "You men will never tarry." And then comes the recognition that she has made a terrible mistake: "O foolish Cressid! I might have still held off,/And then you would have tarried." (17–18) But all this is after the fact, and deep within her, Cressida knows that she is incapable of "holding off," particularly from the man she loves.

This little "morning after" scene can more readily be understood when it is placed alongside the "morning after" scene from *Romeo and Juliet*. In the duet between the young lovers Shakespeare tells us what the real thing is.

> *Juliet.* Wilt thou be gone? It is not yet near day.
> It was the nightingale, and not the lark,
> That pierced the fearful hollow of thine ear.
> Nightly she sings on yond pomegranate tree.
> Believe me, love, it was the nightingale.
> *Romeo.* It was the lark, the herald of the morn;
> No nightingale. Look, love, what envious streaks
> Do lace the severing clouds in yonder East.
> Night's candles are burnt out, and jocund day

Stands tiptoe on the misty mountain tops.
I must be gone and live, or stay and die.
*Juliet.* Yond light is not daylight; I know it, I.
It is some meteor that the sun exhales
To be to thee this night a torchbearer
And light thee on thy way to Mantua.
Therefore stay yet; thou need'st not to be gone.
*Romeo.* Let me be ta'en, let me be put to death.
I am content, so thou wilt have it so.
I'll say yon grey is not the morning's eye,
'Tis but the pale reflex of Cynthia's brow;
Nor that is not the lark whose notes do beat
The vaulty heaven so high above our heads.
I have more care to stay than will to go.
Come, death, and welcome! Juliet wills it so.
How is't, my soul? Let's talk; it is not day.
*Juliet.* It is, it is! Hie hence, be gone, away!
                    (*Romeo and Juliet* III. v.)

Shortly after, the nurse enters.

In *Troilus and Cressida* Pandarus enters to add insult
to injury. Cressida is heartbroken and has to fight off
his obscenities. The scene is interrupted by a loud
knocking on the gate. Cressida's immediate concern is
for Troilus's reputation and she frantically tries to get
him out of sight: "My lord, come you again into my
chamber." Troilus's response to this sincere effort is a
cynical "Ha, ha!" The frantic Cressida, hurt at the
intimation, says:

You smile and mock me, as if I meant naughtily
. . .
Come, you are deceived, I think of no such thing.
How earnestly they knock! Pray you, come in.
I would not for half Troy have you seen here.
                    (37–41)

She means this with all her heart. Troilus permits her to pull him offstage as he mocks her effort.

Aeneas is admitted by Pandarus (44ff.), who feigns ignorance of Troilus's whereabouts. Troilus enters and learns the news that Cressida is to be exchanged for Antenor. His reaction is most interesting and completely predictable. "Is it so concluded?" is all he says. Not a word of protest! Where is the young firebrand who only yesterday, in fact, defied his father, the King, and his elder brother, Hector. He lashed out at them for wanting to end the war by returning Helen to the Greeks. "Why do you . . ./Beggar the estimation which you prized/Richer than sea and land? O theft most base,/ That we have stol'n what we do fear to keep!" We cannot help but recall his rhetoric about taking a wife:

> How may I avoid, [he argued,]
> Although my will distaste what it elected,
> The wife I chose? *There can be no evasion*
> *To blench from this and to stand firm by honor.*
> *We turn not back the silks upon the merchant*
> *When we have soiled them, nor the remainder viands*
> *We do not throw in unrespective sieve*
> *Because we now are full.* (II. ii. 65–72)

How hollow these words sound now that Troilus has soiled the silken Cressida and he is full. Not a word of this. Only "Is it so concluded?" He accepts the edict without a murmur of protest.

If we were to dig a little deeper, we might find that to him the turn of circumstances is not really disturbing, but welcome rather. Though there is no conscious change of feeling on Troilus's part, he is certainly relieved of a situation that, let alone, might become troublesome. Helen is "a theme of honor and renown, A spur to valiant and magnanimous deeds." Helen the

whore is a proper symbol to justify the deaths of so
many men. What of Cressida, whose great fault was
that she gave herself to a man who vowed eternal faith,
a man she loves? Is she not worth fighting for? But all
we get from Troilus is the immediate acceptance of
defeat.

He wallows a little in the lily beds with a few remarks of self pity. He displays little concern for Cressida's plight. He says: "How *my* achievements mock
*me!*" (69) What achievements? A few moments before
he was doing all he could to extricate himself from
Cressida's arms. But now, when separation is forced
upon him, he feels sorry for himself. This is the frame
of mind in which he is happiest. He thrives on frustration and is stimulated by misfortune in "love."

This behavior is quite natural and consistent to
Troilus's character. Koko's song from *The Mikado*
comes to mind. As he gives Yum-Yum up to Nanki-Poo,
he admits:

> Now I adore
> That girl with passion tender
> And could not yield her with a ready will
> Or her allot
> If I did not
> Adore myself with passion tenderer still.

This is Troilus in a nutshell. He is not as honest as the
Lord High Executioner, however.

As Troilus goes sadly out to meet the delegation, an
afterthought strikes him: "And, my Lord Aeneas,/We
met by chance; you did not find me here." (70–71)
Still thinking of his own skin! He might have been
prompted to talk to Cressida first, but, no, she is not
his chief concern at this time.

Pandarus echoes Troilus's concern for Troilus (74ff.).

He, too, has nothing to say about Cressida. "The young prince will go mad" is what bothers him most. He is lamenting as Cressida enters. She knows something terrible has happened. She presses Pandarus for an explanation, "Where's my lord?" she asks, "Gone?" There can be nothing more terrible to Cressida than that "Gone?" Pandarus turns on Cressida with: "Pray thee, get thee in. Would thou hadst ne'er been born! I knew thou wouldst be his death. O poor gentleman!" (87–89) Cressida falls to her knees asking for clarification and Pandarus goes on "attacking her," impervious to the shattered feelings of his niece. "Thou must be gone, *wench*, thou must be gone. . . . Thou must to thy father and be gone from Troilus. 'Twill be his death; 'twill be his bane; he cannot bear it." (91–95)

Cressida's shriek, "O you immortal gods! I will not go," comes from a woman deeply in love and ready to bear any consequences. She comes closest to Juliet in the speech that follows: "But the strong base and building of my love/Is as the very center of the earth,/Drawing all things to it." (105–107) Juliet says:

> My bounty is as boundless as the sea,
> My love as deep; the more I give to thee,
> The more I have, for both are infinite.
> (*Romeo and Juliet* II. ii.)

Juliet can withstand the cruel tricks of fate. She is strong. But more than that, she has Romeo to depend upon. Cressida, who needs the help much more than Juliet, has nobody, has Troilus, who gives nothing.

Cressida insists she will not go from Troy and challenges, "Time, force, and death,/Do to this body what extremes you can. . . ." (103–104) These are the words we should have heard from Troilus. If he had been the man of honor he professed to be, he should have stood

up to Troy's tribunal, and with the same fiery eloquence, refused to let anyone take her. He would have
drawn his sword and threatened to cut down the first
hand that touched his beloved Cressida. "Is it so concluded?" is all we get from him.

Adversity has brought out the best qualities in Cressida. It has given her a strength we did not suspect she
had. She still clings to the idea that Troilus loves her.
There is no doubt in her mind that she loves him. This
gives her strength. We now await the scene between
the two that will put the whole thing to the test and
pave the way for Cressida's "unfaithfulness."

In the meantime, Troilus meets his brother and
Diomedes (IV. iii.). He invites them in and senti-
mentalizes his abominable action:

> I'll bring her to the Grecian presently;
> And to his hand when I deliver her,
> Think it an altar, and thy brother Troilus
> A priest there off'ring to it his own heart.
>
> (6–9)

The images are quite apt since they suggest an innocent
lamb being led to the slaughter. Paris's answer to this is
ironic: "I know what 'tis to love;/And would, as I shall
pity, I could help." Paris cannot help but feel that his
brother is selling out, but since his own position is
precarious enough under the circumstances, he can
hardly be critical.

The scene shifts back to Cressida and Pandarus
(IV. iv.). She is implacable. Her "grief is fine, full,
perfect. . . ." Her love "admits no qualifying dross. . . ."
Troilus enters alone and Cressida rushes into his arms
with, "O Troilus! Troilus!" This simple utterance,
bursting with love and pain, is not the stuff Troilus can

deal with. He veers to his sterile verbiage: "Cressid, I love thee in so strained a purity [purity again],/That the blest gods, as angry with my fancy. . ./Take thee from me." (24–27) He is back in true form once again, words substituting for genuine feelings.

Cressida looks to him for some support, some manifestation of love. (30ff.) She cannot believe that he who made such great promises with such fervor would let her go. "Is it true that I must go from Troy?" Troilus answers, "A hateful truth." She tries again: "What, and from Troilus too?" "From Troy and Troilus," comes the answer. Cressida feels herself falling into an abyss. "Is't possible?" she asks. "And suddenly, . . ." answers Troilus. Cressida's world is collapsing. She barely hears Troilus's prattle on the philosophy and pain of parting, which he mouths in an endless stream of formal verse.

The impatient Aeneas calls, "My lord, is the lady ready?" Cressida is looking at Troilus with unbelieving eyes as Pandarus exits. She notices nothing except Troilus's face; "I must, then, to the Grecians?" again she asks as the realization grows that he will do nothing to stop her departure. "No remedy," says Troilus.

The reality of her situation is upon her and she sees herself, a young attractive woman, alone in the Greek army camp. "A woeful Cressid 'mongst the merry Greeks!" There is a strain of hysteria in this remark. She almost laughs at the thought. But she is suffering deeply. Now she accepts her going, but she doesn't give Troilus up. She still believes in his love when she asks him with tears rolling down her cheeks, "When shall we see again?"

Troilus doesn't answer the question. (58ff.) He has something else on his mind. He is plagued by the thought of Cressida's lying with another man, not because he is in love with her, but for the very reasons

that control his behavior, his preoccupation with "truth
and purity." Would not she who had given in to him
so easily do the same for someone else? He doesn't trust
her. He must exact a promise from her, which he doubts
she will be able to keep. It is his ego that must be satisfied, not his heart. Not being able to understand love,
he fails at this crucial moment to understand a woman
who is in love with him, and who would be unfailing in
her faith were he to trust her and love her.

He begins with "Hear me, love. Be thou but *true*
of heart—" These words are infuriating to Cressida. His
doubt is infuriating. To be untrue had never entered
her mind, but to have her faith questioned at this point
drives her to say: "I true! How now! What wicked
deem is this?" (59) She has turned. This little docile
creature, without a real idea in her head, has turned
on Troilus. He is somewhat taken aback by this response
and tries to worm his way out of the situation with a
circuitous rationale:

> I speak not "be thou *true*" as fearing thee,
> . . .
> But "be thou *true*," say I, to fashion in
> My sequent protestation: be thou *true*,
> And I will see thee.
>
> (62–67)

His explanation softens her reaction for the moment.
More significantly, she becomes concerned about his
safety should he undertake to visit her surreptitiously.
Here is the mark of the true lover. Beset with her own
dangers, far greater than Troilus's, she still says: "O,
you shall be exposed, my lord, to dangers/As infinite
as imminent;" and she adds, "but I'll be true." (68–69)

The moment is a tender one. The erstwhile lovers
exchange tokens. He removes a "sleeve" from his shoul-

der and gives it to her; she takes it and hands him her
glove. It is a painful moment for both of them and she
asks a fearful question, "When shall I see you?" He
replies glibly, "I will corrupt the Grecian sentinels,/To
give thee nightly visitation." But his doubts, which have
never left him, well up once again and he implores,
"But yet, be true."

Cressida's reaction is violent and she pulls away from
him with, "O heavens! 'Be true' again!" The intensity
of her response is evidently conditioned by her own
insecurity and doubts, feelings that at this time need
the greatest kind of support, love, if you will. Instead,
she is fed an adolescent jealousy. Troilus counters with:

> The Grecian youths are full of quality;
> They're loving, well composed with gift of nature,
> And swelling o'er with arts and exercise.
>
> (76–78)

He says this clumsily and he unwittingly introduces the
temptation that Cressida both fears and is attracted to.
But she could have coped with her desires and the difficulty of her situation had Troilus shown confidence in
her and her virtue. But no. His compulsive need for
absolute assurance blinds him to the fact that he is producing a result exactly opposite to what he wants.

Cressida draws the terrifying conclusion: "O heavens,
you love me not!" She moves away, weighing the consequences of this knowledge. (83ff.) Troilus follows her,
trying to make amends, revealing his own sense of in-
feriority in the graces of love-making. Had he stopped
there, which he could not, it might have had some
effect. But he cannot restrain the thought that is eating
away at him, the thought of Cressida possessed by
another man. "Be not tempted," he pleads.

Cressida has grown very still. She looks at Troilus as

at a stranger and asks honestly: "Do you think I will?"
She knows he thinks just that and his overly-protesting
"No!" tells her what she already understands. Troilus
continues, touching the wound with more salt: "But
something may be done that we will not;/And sometimes we are devils to ourselves."

Cressida is quiet and says nothing. Aeneas and Paris,
highly impatient, call out for Troilus. He goes to her:
"Come, kiss; and let us part." She makes no move to
respond to his embrace. "My lord," she says softly, "will
*you* be true?" The meaning of the line is not so much
that she doubts the fact that Troilus will remain pure.
It is a woman's question in a man's world. Coming
from Cressida, it shows a mark of maturity. It is related
to Emilia's talk with Desdemona in *Othello*. It is a
challenge of the double standard.

> But I do think it is their husbands' faults
> If wives do fall . . .
> Why, we have galls . . . Let husbands know
> Their wives have sense like them. They see, and smell,
> And have their palates both for sweet and sour,
> As husbands have.
>
> (*Othello* IV. iii. 95ff.)

(Is it a coincidence that *Othello* comes shortly after
*Troilus and Cressida* in the canon? I think not. In this
period Shakespeare was exploring the relationships of
men and women within a society organized according
to a male code of behavior.)

Troilus answers with all sincerity that he is incapable
of being false to her. If this is true, then fidelity is no
problem for him. One may wish to comment that there
is something missing in a man totally free of temptation. Be this as it may, the fact that he is making a
demand on Cressida to behave in a manner that for him

requires no effort, and even further prohibits the behavior in her he most recently encouraged, is the height
of selfishness. Cressida must make all the sacrifices.

Troilus does give an accurate estimation of his inbred
"purity." "Alas," he cries, "it is my vice, my fault."
Here he echoes a reply he had made the night before
to Cressida when she had held him off with: "They say
all lovers swear more performance than they are able."
He had answered: "Such are not we. Praise us as we are
tasted, allow us as we prove; *our head shall go bare till
merit crown it.*" (III. ii. 92–94)

He continues to damn himself with praise:

> Whiles others fish with craft for great opinion,
> I with *great truth* catch mere simplicity;
> Whilst some with cunning gild their copper crowns,
> With *truth* and plainness *I do wear mine bare.*
> Fear not my *truth*; the moral of my wit
> Is "plain *and true*"—there's all the reach of it.
> (103–108)

All of Troilus's words in this scene abound with un-
conscious sexual connotations. While he warns Cressida
against temptation, he is filling her ears with images
and sounds that provoke in her the thing he fears. He
talks of the Greeks as "swelling o'er with arts and exercise"; they (the Greeks) "are most prompt and pregnant"; in each of them "there lurks a still and dumb-
discursive devil." He speaks of tempting "the frailty of
our powers" and their "changeful potency." And finally,
he talks of fishing and Greek heads that are cunningly
gilded in contrast to his own.

Unconsciously he is doing the job of seduction and
enticement for Diomedes, the Greek, who enters precisely at this moment. He couldn't have better prepared
Cressida for Diomedes, were he Pandarus himself.

(109ff.) "Welcome, Sir Diomed," says Troilus. Welcome indeed. "Here is the lady. . . ./At the port, lord, I'll give her to thy hand,/ And by the way *possess thee what she is*." Diomedes brushes aside Troilus's admonition to "Entreat her fair. . . ." He has already caught a glimpse of her and she of him. He moves directly to her, playing the role exactly as Troilus had just described it. "Fair Lady Cressid," he says, "So please you, save the thanks this prince expects."

> The luster in your eye, heaven in your cheek,
> Pleads your fair *usage*; and to Diomed
> *You shall be mistress.* . . .
>
> (118–120)

He uses the word "mistress" in its double connotation.

Troilus lashes out impotently at Diomedes, who knows he holds the superior position. Cressida's tear-stained face tells him everything. And further, he is disdainful of a prince who could permit his woman to be turned over to someone else, high-sounding phrases notwithstanding. During this dialogue Cressida is silent. It is all over between her and Troilus. She knows it. He does not.

Troilus threatens Diomedes with words that the latter can hardly neglect to take advantage of: "I charge thee," says Troilus, "*use her* well." That is exactly what the Greek is determined to do. Diomedes' easy and confident answer is a precursor of the events to follow:

> O, be not moved, Prince Troilus. . . .
>                          When I am hence,
> I'll answer to my lust; . . . To her own worth
> She shall be prized. . . .
>
> (129ff.)

Troilus can only threaten; the only proper thing to do, which he cannot, is to refuse to let Cressida go. All the men present—Paris, Aeneas, Antenor, and Deiphobus—watch him dishonor himself before the enemy. They are silent in the shame of it. Troilus at this moment is a tragic figure. He is caught in the web of his own nature, which prevents him from breaking out of it. It is this helplessness that wins him the sympathy of the audience, but it should not win him its forgiveness.

To Diomedes' challenge, Troilus can only promise to settle the score in the future: "I'll tell thee, Diomed,/ This brave shall oft make thee to hide thy head." (136–137) Here Troilus is in his element: fighting, war. The terms of warfare are simple and direct. Anyway, Troilus finds it much easier to hate an enemy than to love a woman. In an interesting way, the challenge to Diomedes helps Troilus out of an embarrassing situation; he is on familiar ground. He turns his back on the unconcerned Diomedes and turns to Cressida.

Cressida has been motionless since she asked the question: "My lord, will you be true?" Now she picks up her cloak and waits to be commanded. Troilus asks for her hand, but he is forced to take it as they exit, followed by Diomedes and Antenor. They head for the city's gates, through the quiet streets.

Paris, Aeneas, and Deiphobus stay on, embarrassed to look at one another. They are saved by the sound of Hector's trumpet. Action is the answer. "How have we spent this morning!" says Aeneas. Paris's rejoinder, " 'Tis Troilus' fault," is a cynical one and Aeneas catches the tone as they all leave the stage.

Although Troilus had said: "and, as we walk,/To our own selves bend we our needful talk," Cressida has

passed the talking stage. Shakespeare has given her a
long, long silence. Let us try to "roll the camera back"
to the events of the morning after, eliminating all lines
but Cressida's.

*Cressida.*

Are you aweary of me?

Prithee, tarry;
You men will never tarry.
O foolish Cressid! I might have still held off,
And then you would have tarried.

Go hang yourself, you naughty mocking uncle.
You bring me to do, and then you flout me too.

My lord, come you again into my chamber.
You smile and mock me, as if I meant naughtily.

Come, you are deceived, I think of no such thing. . .
I would not for half Troy have you seen here.

O you immortal gods! I will not go.

I will not, uncle. I have forgot my father. . .
No kin, no love, no blood, no soul so near me
As the sweet Troilus. O you gods divine,
Make Cressid's name the very crown of falsehood
If ever she leave Troilus! Time, force, and death,
Do to this body what extremes you can;
But the strong base and building of my love
Is as the very center of the earth,
Drawing all things to it. I will go in and weep—

—Tear my bright hair, and scratch my praisèd cheeks,
Crack my clear voice with sobs, and break my heart
With sounding Troilus. I will not go from Troy.

Why tell you me of moderation?
The grief is fine, full, perfect, that I taste. . .
My love admits no qualifying dross;
No more my grief, in such a precious loss.

O Troilus! Troilus!

Have the gods envy?

And is it true that I must go from Troy?

What, and from Troilus too?

Is't possible?

I must, then, to the Grecians?

A woeful Cressid 'mongst the merry Greeks!
When shall we see again?

I true! How now! What wicked deem is this?

O, you shall be exposed, my lord, to dangers
As infinite as imminent; but I'll be true.

When shall I see you?

O heavens! 'Be true' again!

O heavens, you love me not!

Do you think I will?

My lord, will you be true?

It is revealing to analyze Cressida's emotional development and trace the process of her growth as a character. Unlike Troilus, who shows promise but no fulfillment, Cressida begins her life in the play confused, uncertain, and fearful. This leads her to behave and speak in a pseudo-sophisticated and superficial manner; to engage in sexual banter in order to cover her anxieties; to adopt a philosophy of cunning common sense to ward off the pressures of her uncle and of Troilus; and to tease and flirt for the same reason. She is a little girl trying to act the woman of the world; actually, she is an inexperienced girl without a family or friend. All these defenses are broken down after the night she spends with Troilus. Without them she becomes utterly helpless.

It is not what Troilus has given her that makes her vulnerable and dependent, but what he has taken away. And we are not discussing maidenheads, but Cressida's way of coping with her life. She has nothing else but her defenses for support. Without those props, she cannot stand alone. Yes, Troilus was her first love—the first man she gave herself to—and nobody will deny the emotional consequences of this experience. Her desperation at the thought of parting is founded on more than "love." It is a combination of real and subjective circumstances that manifest themselves in such horrendous outcries as: "I have forgot my father. . ./ No kin, no love, no blood, no soul so near me/As the sweet Troilus. . . ./Tear my bright hair, and scratch my praisèd cheeks,/Crack my clear voice with sobs, and break my heart/With sounding Troilus." (IV. iii. 98–111)

These are cries of great pain and fear. She is now capable of doing what Juliet did, that is, commit suicide, and she would do it gladly if Troilus had suggested this way out. Troilus's support is vital to her, but his words are devoid of hope; they turn Cressida to stone right before our eyes; and her silence is a silence bred of dead hopes and a dead future. From the line "O heavens, you love me not," the process of petrification

begins its course through her body. By the time she says
"My lord, will you be true?" she's older and wiser and
cynical.

When Diomedes walks in she sizes him up coolly.
There is an immediate understanding. Diomedes is the
kind of man who will fulfill his masculine obligations
and responsibilities. Cressida has a sense of this.

It is entirely possible that en route to the city gates,
not a single word passed the lips of Cressida. Troilus is
left with the image of Cressida walking alongside of
Diomedes toward the Grecian tents. He may have seen
Diomedes lift her by the waist to an Arabian charger
and then mount his own steed. We may also consider
that Cressida maintained her frozen silence for the entire ride. Diomedes, in deference to her feelings, trots
quietly a few paces behind. His eyes are on her hair.

Shakespeare does not tell us what happens between
Cressida and Diomedes on their way to the Greek camp.
We may guess that the great silence of Cressida is maintained, that Diomedes wisely refrains from intruding on
her grief. He is probably courteous and considerate,
mindful of her comfort. He knows that it is just a
matter of time before he'll have her and that her feelings
must run their course.

Following the sad parting scene, Shakespeare plunges
us into a noisy farcical situation in the Greek camp.
(IV. v.) The clumsy Ajax, fully armed, and still being
touted by the conspirators, performs a comic routine
with a trumpeter. In the midst of this, Agamemnon
sees Diomedes and Cressida approaching. Ulysses' description of the approaching Diomedes is a magnificent
capsule character summary. But Shakespeare is not content with a single brilliant stroke. He lets us know also
that Ulysses doesn't like Diomedes. Ulysses observes, as
he watches Diomedes approach,

I ken the manner of his gait;
He rises on the toe. That spirit of his
In aspiration lifts him from the earth.

(14–16)

All eyes are turned on Cressida as she walks into the
Greek camp. Diomedes, the perfect soldier, stands to
one side as his commander approaches. Agamemnon
eyes her with great relish. "Is this the Lady Cressid?"
She is more beautiful than they had expected, and for
men engaged in war for more than five years, her arrival
is an unexpected treat. The atmosphere is charged with
male lust. After all, the issue in the war is a whore. All
principals in the struggle are contaminated by the sickness of the cause. And here is a lovely creature, in an
army camp, her only "protector" a traitorous father to
whom they feel very little obligation. There is an un-
conscious connecting of father and daughter. Since he
can sell out, why not she?

As Cressida walks the gauntlet of men, all we can
hear is heavy breathing. All want her. What ensues is
a kind of rape scene. The kiss is a substitute for sexual
assault, but the effect is no less devastating. All the
characters play out their own frustrations through
Cressida. Cressida is tossed about from man to man
and she offers no resistance. She cynically accepts the
role of harlot conferred upon her by Troilus. Not only
does she accept the part, but she plays it to the hilt.
Here is the Cressida of the first scene with this addition:
the allusions to men and sex, earlier in the play only in
her fantasy, now exist in an equally fantastic reality.

Agamemnon starts with a hard kiss on Cressida's
mouth, but it is Ulysses who gives the signal for the
attack. Old Nestor, drooling at the mouth, says, "Our
general doth salute you with a kiss." (19) Ulysses' contempt for women calls forth his speech, "Yet is the

kindness but particular./'Twere better she were kissed in general." (20–21) Nestor needs no further prodding. He begins. Achilles pulls her away from the ancient oracle and plants a rough and dirty kiss on Cressida's mouth. Menelaus, the "oblique memorial of cuckolds," catches Cressida as Achilles throws her aside and tries to embrace her. But Patroclus intervenes with "thus popped Paris in his hardiment,/And parted thus you and your argument." He kisses her twice as the cynical Ulysses shows his contempt for Menelaus with: "O, deadly gall, and theme of all our scorns,/For which we lose our heads to gild his horns." (30–31) Menelaus is persistent. He needs that kiss desperately. He pleads for it, but Cressida plays cruelly with his desires. She is learning the game, the Helen game.

As we examine her remarks we find they stem from her disillusionment with Troilus. She recklessly engages Menelaus with telling lines (36ff.): "In kissing, do you render or receive?" Troilus *received*, but did not *render*. "I'll make my match to live." A bet she can make with confidence based on her experience. "The kiss you *take* is better than you *give*." Her kiss to Troilus was better than he gave. She gave hers with love; his was not sincere.

"Therefore no kiss." A taunt seductively delivered. Sex is her weapon and she can employ it to make men crawl. She rejects Menelaus's offer of three kisses for one. Her pun "give even, or give none" implies that her kisses henceforth are only available on an equal basis.

Giving and taking, rendering and receiving, is the new theme of Cressida's outlook. The play on words, and the manner of delivery do not conceal the bitterness underlying them. From now on, men will have to beg for it. She too can play the Helen game.

Ulysses' hatred of Helen, a feeling he has always kept under control, now erupts. He moves into the game

that he understands so well. Ulysses is out for blood as
he takes Menelaus out of the way. He acts the gallant
with "May I, sweet lady, beg a kiss of you?" Cressida
senses the enemy and engages him.

> *Cressida.* You may [beg].
> *Ulysses.* [feigning helplessness] I do desire it.
> *Cressida.*                              Why, beg then.
> *Ulysses.* Why, then, for Venus's sake, give me a kiss,
>     When Helen is a maid again, and his.
>
>                              [i.e., Menelaus's]
>                              (48–50)

Since Helen can never be a maid again, Ulysses tells
Cressida she can keep her kiss. He doesn't want any
part of it. But Cressida retaliates, "I am your debtor;
claim it when 'tis due." Ulysses doesn't waste any more
words in banter. He tells her straight out, "Never's my
day, and then a kiss for you."

This exchange might have led to further complica-
tions, but Diomedes rescues her (something Troilus did
not do). In virtual defiance of his superiors, he takes
her away from the hungry mob, and particularly from
the sharp disdainful clutches of Ulysses.

> *Diomedes.* Lady, a word. I'll bring you to your father.

Cressida was correct in her appraisal of him.

Old Nestor's comment of appreciation as she is leaving is put down by the furious Ulysses.

> *Nestor.* A woman of quick sense.
> *Ulysses.*                              Fie, fie upon her!
>     There's language in her eye, her cheek, her lip;
>     Nay, her foot speaks. Her wanton spirits look out
>     At every joint and motive of her body.
>                              (54–57)

The warriors listen to Ulysses' attack on "daughters of the game," but they, like he, want it no other way.

On the large stage of the Delacorte Theater, actors' exits are prolonged. There is some value, however, in the limitation. In the case of Cressida leaving the stage with Diomedes, we hear Ulysses' speech about her while she is still in motion. It is interesting to observe her walking off as Ulysses characterizes her movement: "Nay, her foot speaks. Her wanton spirits look out/At every joint and motive of her body." By the time Ulysses reaches the end of his speech six lines later, she is gone, and we hear the Trojan trumpet and see Troilus approaching.

Here again, Shakespeare's technique of overlapping themes is admirably demonstrated here. Note the extraordinary interplay of major and minor "sounds." In this respect, the scene is a capsule version of the entire play. Following the trumpet blast that sets the militaristic tone of the scene, we hear the loud words of challenge, visually supported by two contending armies with flags, banners, and weapons. On the surface is the pending fight between Hector and Ajax. Ajax is chafing at the bit, but somewhat nervous at the prospect of facing so honored an opponent. Hector is relaxed and smiling as he weighs his weapon with professional carelessness. He is somewhat amused at his cousin's intensity. This is theme one. But there is a variation here, supplied by Achilles, who tries to appear unconcerned but who watches Hector's every look and motion. His presence is not unobserved by Hector, who pretends to ignore him. Patroclus fearfully watches Achilles, his brooding lover, adding another note to the composition. Still another variation is provided by the exchange of glances of Helen's pitiful husband, Menelaus, with her

lover and abductor, Paris. But it is Troilus who con-
tributes the subtle, yet dominant, strain. He is looking
for Cressida. His mind is not on immediate matters.

The audience has not yet disconnected itself from the
exit of Diomedes and Cressida. And at the moment that
this strain is about to be lost, Diomedes returns. In our
staging we provided passing contact between Diomedes
and Troilus, which brought that theme into sharp focus.
Shakespeare keeps the Diomedes-Troilus note "under"
the entire scene. After the confrontation of Achilles and
Hector, this note reappears in strength.

Ulysses is made part of this theme by his glowing
description of Troilus, in contrast to his earlier disprais-
ing of Diomedes. Agamemnon asks, "What Troyan
is that same that looks so heavy?" Ulysses' answer must
be understood in the context of his objectives and feelings. We have just listened to his wrathful condemnation of Cressida (so unlike his faithful Penelope), and
we have heard his contempt for Diomedes. These were
personal prejudices. Ulysses has no objection to turning
them into instruments of policy. He is fully attuned to
what is going on between Troilus and Diomedes and
hopes to aggravate the condition at the appropriate
time. His eyes are on Troilus. Here is the man who can
and will be goaded to provoke an all-out battle between
the Greeks and the Trojans, something Ulysses considers militarily desirable. Therefore, the answer to
Agamemnon's question should be seen in the light of
Ulysses' purposes.

*Ulysses.* The youngest son of Priam, a true knight,
   Not yet mature, yet matchless; firm of word,
   Speaking in deeds and deedless in his tongue,
   Not soon provoked, nor being provoked soon calmed;
   His heart and hand both open and both free,

For what he has he gives, what thinks he shows;
Yet gives he not till judgment guide his bounty,
Nor dignifies an impure thought with breath;
Manly as Hector, but more dangerous;
For Hector, in his blaze of wrath, subscribes
To tender objects, but he in heat of action
Is more vindicative than jealous love.
They call him Troilus, and on him erect
A second hope as fairly built as Hector.
Thus says Aeneas, one that knows the youth
Even to his inches, and with private soul
Did in great Ilion thus translate him to me.
(96–112)

There is irony in this description. "Firm of word" is
Troilus. Yet he has so recently broken his vow to
Cressida. But when Ulysses says he is more dangerous
than Hector because "in heat of action [he]/Is more
vindicative than jealous love," the description is apt.
Ulysses is disdainful of Hector's subscription "to tender
objects." This kind of sportsmanship, in Ulysses' thinking, stands in the way of an all-out battle, which he
believes the Greeks could win.

The contest over, and the confrontation of Achilles
and Hector ending in a challenge, all are invited to
Agamemnon's tent for feasting and drinking. Diomedes
is anxious to get back to Cressida, but he must fulfill his
military obligations first. Troilus's presence heightens
this desire. All leave the stage except Troilus, who,
sensing a sympathetic figure in the Greek general, stops
Ulysses. Troilus has just seen Diomedes leaving and
suspects that he is headed for Cressida. Although he is
desperate, Troilus manages to conceal his feelings with
a casual question, "My Lord Ulysses, tell me, I beseech

you,/In what place of the field doth Calchas keep?"
(276–277) Ulysses' answer is full of deliberate provoca-
tion. He tells the place, but he adds the ingredients that
turn to bile in Troilus's stomach:

> There Diomed doth feast with him tonight—
> Who neither looks upon the heaven nor earth,
> But gives all gaze and bent of amorous view
> On the fair Cressid.
>
> (279–282)

Troilus, in agony, but restrained and superbly courteous,
asks Ulysses to show him the way after the feast.

Ulysses wants nothing better than that, but he is not
content to stop here. He feigns a paternal concern for
the boy, "But *gentle* tell me, of what honor was/This
Cressida in Troy? Had she no lover there/That wails
her absence?" Here we have Ulysses at his hypocritical
best. Honor is for babies, and people are puppets to be
manipulated for his own ends. He began with a scheme
to move Achilles into action, using Ajax as the decoy.
Now he has Troilus and will use him.

Troilus's reply is pathetic. Yet it is interesting that
the pain he is feeling makes his words somewhat simpler
though not entirely free of sentimental romanticism.
"She was beloved, she loved; she is, and doth;/But still
sweet love is food for fortune's tooth." (291–292) "Fortune's tooth"—not pretty, but apt.

The "movement" is not over yet. As we look back
we discover that, amazingly, all that has transpired in
the play covers a time period of only two days. We are
now entering the second night of the second day.
*Troilus and Cressida* has in actuality one great movement that begins in Act I, Scene i with Troilus's desir-
ing Cressida, and ends in Act V, Scene ii at the final
disillusionment of the lovers. The last eight scenes of

the play represent an epilogue of dissonance, a mixture of the tragic and absurd, played out in a wild cacophonous dance of death and destruction.

Shakespeare prepares us for the final scene involving Troilus and Cressida by first contaminating the atmosphere. For this purpose, he utilizes the brooding and murderous Achilles and his male varlet, Patroclus. (V. i.) Achilles' paranoiac torment can only be eased by the death of Hector. His venomous yearnings brim over with desire and hatred for the great Hector. Patroclus is painfully aware of this ambivalence, sees it as a threat to their relationship and is, therefore, uncertain of his own feelings over the promised encounter. There is the possibility of Achilles being killed in the fight. However, he is elated over the prospect of the other possibility, Hector's demise.

It is Thersites, however, who is Shakespeare's chief instrument of contamination. In his vituperative spewing in this scene he is the scenic painter who creates the ugly background for the ugly events to follow. He fills the stage with:

> . . . rotten diseases of the south, the guts-griping ruptures, catarrhs, loads o' gravel in the back, lethargies, cold palsies, raw eyes, dirt-rotten livers, wheezing lungs, bladders full of imposthume, sciaticas, lime-kilns i' the palm, incurable bone-ache. . . .
>
> (17–22)

And as Achilles and Patroclus exit, he launches into a tirade against the great heroes of the war, Agamemnon and his brother, Menelaus, "a thrifty shoeing-horn in a chain, hanging at his brother's leg. . . ."[2]

---

[2] See *Production Notes* for stage version of this phrase.

The growing madness of events is heightened by the entrance of Agamemnon, Ulysses, Nestor, Hector, Ajax, Menelaus, Diomedes, and Troilus. The Greek general is drunk and so are Nestor, Ajax, and Menelaus. Hector is slightly intoxicated. But Ulysses, Troilus, and Diomedes are stone sober. Thersites conceals himself and watches the merrymakers with contempt.

Troilus hears Diomedes' reply to Achilles' invitation to enter his tent: "I cannot, lord; I have important business,/The tide whereof is now." As Diomedes leaves, Ulysses instructs Troilus to "Follow his torch; he goes to Calchas's tent." Thersites is left alone on the stage to give us his evaluation of Diomedes' character, "a false-hearted rogue, a most unjust knave." He calls him a liar. "I will no more trust him when he leers than I will a serpent when he hisses." Shakespeare needs Thersites in the scene that is to follow. "I'll after," says Thersites, "—nothing but lechery! All incontinent varlets!"

The reunion scene (V. ii.) of Cressida and her father, Calchas, takes place off-stage. But the one-line answer Calchas gives to Diomedes' query, "Where's your daughter?" "She comes to you." tells the story without any needed elaboration. He will play the role of pimp for his own child.

Ulysses and Troilus conceal themselves on one side of the stage, Thersites on the other, but further downstage. The "love scene" will occupy center stage.

Cressida appears and goes to Diomedes. She has already decided not to keep her promise to Troilus. She goes about conveying this decision in a teasing and playful way, reminiscent of the first time we saw her. The one significant difference is that she is playing the game with greater assurance and cynicism. Ulysses continues his role of provocateur with his comment that Cressida "will sing any man at first sight." Thersites chimes in with an obscenity, indicative of his counter-point role in the scene.

Her toying angers Diomedes, who threatens to leave, but she lures him back again, and whispers caressingly in his ear. Troilus watches the agonizing procedure as Ulysses goads him and restrains him at the same time.

Cressida teases Diomedes again with promises. She has actually won a reprieve. But Diomedes' frustration requires a stronger commitment. He asks "some token for the surety of it." Cressida goes back into her father's tent and returns with the sleeve given to her by Troilus. The sight of this enrages Troilus beyond all measure, but Ulysses holds him back.

No sooner does Cressida give the sleeve to Diomedes than she snatches it back. Diomedes insists on knowing to whom the sleeve belonged. Cressida has a moment of conscience and she says, "I will not meet with you tomorrow night./I prithee, Diomed, visit me no more." Diomedes, his appetite sharpened by her teasing, tries to grab the sleeve from her hand. She responds, "O, all you gods! O pretty, pretty pledge!" (74) The sleeve has become the symbol of her girlhood innocence. Giving it up will be the beginning of a long and unending road of men. She looks at the sleeve, her eyes filling with tears:

> Thy master now lies thinking on his bed
> Of thee and me, and sighs, and takes my glove,
> And gives memorial dainty kisses to it,
> As I kiss thee.

Diomedes savagely pulls the sleeve from her hand.

> Nay, do not snatch it from me;
> *He that takes that doth take my heart withal.*
> (75–79)

Diomedes replies, "I had your heart before; this follows
it." Since Cressida will not name Troilus as her lover,
Diomedes tells her, "Tomorrow will I wear it on my
helm,/And grieve his spirit that dares not challenge it."
(90–91) Cressida makes a few more futile gestures of
defiance, then submits. When he threatens to leave
once more, she returns to her feminine wiles:

> You shall not go. One cannot speak a word
> But it straight starts you.
> *Diomedes.*                I do not like this fooling.

When Diomedes asks for a plain answer, she replies at
last:

>                          Ay, come—O Jove!—
> Do come—I shall be plagued.
> *Diomedes.*                Farewell till then.
> *Cressida.* Good night. I prithee, come.
>                          (97–103)

Diomedes leaves and Cressida is heard for the last time.
She speaks of being torn between Troilus and Diomedes. "Minds swayed by eyes are full of turpitude." *baseless*
  The conflict is not really in her choice of the two *depravity*
men, but of two situations. The first, with Troilus, is
impossible. The second, with Diomedes, is a reality she
must face. The key phrase in her last speech can be
found in this cry, "*ah, poor our sex!*" That is more to
the point. Cressida is a victim of men, their wars, their
desires, and their double standards. Thersites' remark
that follows her exit is the male point of view, and was
undoubtedly applauded by the Elizabethan audience.
"A proof of strength she could not publish more,/
Unless she said, 'My mind is now turned whore.' "
(110–111) The Central Park audience responded in

like manner. The women in the audience were quiet
during the scene. Many of the men guffawed.

The principal male actors of the company shared
Thersites' view of Cressida. In particular, the actor playing Troilus raised the question in this way: "Why did
she give Diomedes the sleeve if she was not a faithless
slut?" The actress playing Cressida provided the answer.
"I could not be untrue to Troilus and retain the token
of his love. That would be immoral. I had to free myself
honorably from the previous vow." Since circumstances
forced her into a situation beyond her control, she did
the "honorable" thing.

Troilus feels no responsibility for the events. He attacks her "infidelity":

> The bonds of heaven are slipped, dissolved, and
>     loosed, [Bonds of heaven, indeed, tied by a
>     pander in a casual night in bed???]
> And with another knot, five-finger-tied,
> The fractions of her faith, orts of her love,
> The fragments, scraps, the bits, and greasy relics
> Of her o'ereaten faith, are given to Diomed.
>                                     (153–157)

His rantings are interrupted by Aeneas with the news of
the impending battle. They leave. Only Thersites stays
on to comment, "Lechery, lechery; still wars and lechery; nothing else holds fashion. A burning devil take
them!" (192–193)

The story of Troilus and Cressida is ended. All that
remains to be seen is the cruel death of Hector and
Troilus's vow of revenge. History has the final answer,
however. Troy is foredoomed to a bloody end.

To dispel any doubts of his intentions, Shakespeare,
at the height of the tragedy, brings Pandarus forth to
end the play. He talks to the audience, calls them

"traders in the flesh," "breathren and sisters of the hold-door trade," and bequeaths them his diseases. (V. x. 35ff.) The playwright makes it known that the corruption they have witnessed on the stage is not limited to the characters of the play.

THE FESTIVAL SHAKESPEARE

*Troilus and Cressida*

Produced by JOSEPH PAPP

IN COOPERATION WITH THE CITY OF NEW YORK

Hon. ROBERT F. WAGNER, *Mayor*

Hon. NEWBOLD MORRIS, *Commissioner of Parks*

PRESENTS WILLIAM SHAKESPEARE'S

# TROILUS AND CRESSIDA

Directed by JOSEPH PAPP    Setting by MING CHO LEE
Lighting by MARTIN ARONSTEIN    Costumes by THEONI V. ALDREDGE
Music by DAVID AMRAM    Swordplay by JAMES J. SLOYAN

## THE CAST

| | | |
|---|---|---|
| PRIAM, *King of Troy* | ............... | Leonard Hicks |
| HECTOR | ⎫ | Paul Stevens |
| TROILUS | ⎪ | Richard Jordan |
| PARIS | *his sons* | Humbert Alan Astredo |
| DEIPHOBUS | ⎪ | Peter Jacob |
| HELENUS | ⎪ | Michael Moriarty |
| MARGARELON | ⎭ | James Howard |
| AENEAS | *Trojan commanders* | Jack Ryland |
| ANTENOR | | Morris Erby |
| CALCHAS, *a priest, father to Cressida* | ... | John Hetherington |
| PANDARUS, *uncle to Cressida* | ........ | Frank Schofield |
| AGAMEMNON, *the Greek General* | .. | Gerald E. McGonagill |
| MENELAUS, *his brother* | ......... | Michael McGuire |
| ACHILLES | ⎫ | John Vernon |
| AJAX | ⎪ | James Earl Jones |
| ULYSSES | *Greek commanders* | Roscoe Lee Browne |
| NESTOR | ⎪ | Tom Aldredge |
| DIOMEDES | ⎪ | Al Freeman, Jr. |
| PATROCLUS | ⎭ | Bill Gunn |
| THERSITES, *a servant to Ajax, later to Achilles* | | |
| | | Joseph Bova |
| HELEN, *wife to Menelaus* | .......... | Jane White |
| CASSANDRA, *daughter to Priam* | ...... | Tobi Weinberg |
| ANDROMACHE, *wife to Hector* | ....... | Chase Crosley |
| CRESSIDA, *daughter to Calchas* | ....... | Flora Elkins |
| ALEXANDER, *servant to Cressida* | ..... | Seymour Penzner |
| SERVANT to Troilus | .............. | James Arnold |
| SERVANT to Paris | ............... | Robert Ronan |
| SERVANT to Diomedes | ........... | Peter Yoshida |
| MYRMIDON | ............... | Ronald Johnson |

*Soldiers and Attendants*: Burke Byrnes, Festus Collier, Oliver Dixon, John Genke, Alex Healy, John Hoffmeister, Leonard Jackson, Philip Kroopf, George McGrath, George Muschamp, Nat Simmons, John Starr, John Vidette, Lisle Wilson.

*Musicians*: Andrew J. Baron, Richard Berg, Henry J. Nowak.

SCENE: TROY, AND THE GREEK CAMP
*There will be one fifteen-minute intermission.*

Associate Producer—BERNARD GERSTEN

# A Note on the Text

The present edition, based on the 1609 Quarto and modified slightly according to the Folio copy, contains a complete text of the play. Passages omitted in the New York Shakespeare Festival production are marked by parentheses. Editorial additions, most of which have been handed down by successive editors, are enclosed in square brackets. Notes on aspects of the production are indicated by asterisks.

*Troilus.* And when fair Cressid comes into my thoughts—.
*(I.i.32) Left to right: Pandarus, Troilus*

*Thersites*. Thou canst strike, canst thou? A red murrain o' thy jade's tricks!
(II.i.19–20) *Left to right: Ajax, Thersites*

*Helen.* Falling in, after falling out, may make them three.
(*III.i.104–105*) *Left to right: Paris, Helen, Pandarus*

GEORGE E. JOSEPH

*Pandarus.* Let all constant men be Troiluses, all false women
Cressids, and all brokers-between Pandars!
*(III.ii.204–205) Left to right: Cressida, Pandarus, Troilus*

*Pandarus.* Let me embrace too. "O heart," as the goodly saying is—

> O heart, heavy heart,
> Why sigh'st thou without breaking?

(IV.iv.14–17) *Left to right: Pandarus, Troilus, Cressida (behind Troilus)*

*Menelaus.* I'll have my kiss, sir. Lady, by your leave.
*(IV.v.35) Left to right: Ajax, Agamemnon, Patroclus, Cressida, Nestor (behind Cressida), Menelaus, Ulysses, Diomedes*

*Achilles.* So, Ilion, fall thou next! Come, Troy, sink down!
Here lies thy heart, thy sinews, and thy bone.
*(V.viii.11–12) Left to right: Myrmidons (in helmets), Achilles (bareheaded), Hector (being speared)*

GEORGE E. JOSEPH

*Troilus.*                  Hector is gone.
Who shall tell Priam so, or Hecuba?
Let him that will a screech owl aye be called
Go in to Troy, and say there Hector's dead.
*(V.x.14–17) Trojan soldiers left, Troilus right*

# Troilus and Cressida

## THE PROLOGUE

[*Enter the Prologue in armor.*]*

In Troy there lies the scene. From isles of Greece
The princes orgulous, their high blood chafed,
Have to the port of Athens sent their ships,
Fraught with the ministers and instruments
Of cruel war. Sixty and nine, that wore                          5
Their crownets regal, from th' Athenian bay
Put forth toward Phrygia; and their vow is made
To ransack Troy, within whose strong immures
The ravished Helen, Menelaus' queen,
With wanton Paris sleeps—and that's the quarrel.                10
To Tenedos they come,
And the deep-drawing barks do there disgorge
Their warlike fraughtage. Now on Dardan plains
The fresh and yet unbruisèd Greeks do pitch
Their brave pavilions. Priam's six-gated city,                  15
Dardan, and Timbria, Helias, Chetas, Troien,
And Antenorides, with massy staples
And corresponsive and fulfilling bolts,
Sperr up the sons of Troy.
Now expectation, tickling skittish spirits,                     20

Prologue 2 *orgulous* proud    7 *Phrygia* western Asia Minor    8 *immures* walls    11 *Tenedos* the port of Troy    13 *fraughtage* cargo, i.e., of soldiers    13 *Dardan* Trojan    15 *brave* splendid    16–17 *Dardan . . . Antenorides* names of the gates of Troy    18 *fulfilling* filling tightly    19 *Sperr up* shut up

On one and other side, Troyan and Greek,
Sets all on hazard. And hither am I come,
A prologue armed, but not in confidence
Of author's pen or actor's voice, but suited
In like conditions as our argument,     25
To tell you, fair beholders, that our play
Leaps o'er the vaunt and firstlings of those broils,
Beginning in the middle, starting thence away
To what may be digested in a play.
Like or find fault; do as your pleasures are;     30
Now good or bad, 'tis but the chance of war.

23 *armed* in armor    24 *suited* dressed    25 *argument* subject, i.e.,
of the story    27 *vaunt* van, first part

## ~§ ACT I. i §~

[*Troy. A street near one of the gates.*]*

*Enter Pandarus and Troilus.*

TROILUS. Call here my varlet, I'll unarm again.
Why should I war without the walls of Troy
That find such cruel battle here within?
Each Troyan* that is master of his heart,
Let him to field; Troilus, alas, hath none.                    5
PANDARUS. Will this gear ne'er be mended?
TROILUS. The Greeks are strong, and skillful to their
        strength,
Fierce to their skill, and to their fierceness valiant;
But I am weaker than a woman's tear,
Tamer than sleep, fonder than ignorance,                       10
Less valiant than the virgin in the night,
And skilless as unpracticed infancy.
PANDARUS. Well, I have told you enough of this. For
my part, I'll not meddle nor make no farther. He
that will have a cake out of the wheat must tarry     15
the grinding.
TROILUS. Have I not tarried?
PANDARUS. Ay, the grinding; but you must tarry the
bolting.
TROILUS. Have I not tarried?                                   20
PANDARUS. Ay, the bolting; but you must tarry the
leavening.
TROILUS. Still have I tarried.
PANDARUS. Ay, to the leavening; but here's yet in the
word "hereafter" the kneading, the making of the     25
cake, the heating the oven, and the baking. Nay,

I.i.1 *varlet* servant    6 *gear* business    7 *to* in addition to    10
*fonder* more foolish    19 *bolting* sifting

you must stay the cooling too, or ye may chance
burn your lips.

TROILUS. Patience herself, what goddess e'er she be,
Doth lesser blench at suff'rance than I do.          30
At Priam's royal table do I sit,
And when fair Cressid comes into my thoughts—
So, traitor, when she comes! When is she thence?

PANDARUS. Well, she looked yesternight fairer than
ever I saw her look, or any woman else.          36

TROILUS. I was about to tell thee, when my heart,
As wedgèd with a sigh, would rive in twain,
Lest Hector or my father should perceive me—
I have, as when the sun doth light a-scorn,
Buried this sigh in wrinkle of a smile;          40
(But sorrow, that is couched in seeming gladness,
Is like that mirth fate turns to sudden sadness.)

PANDARUS. An her hair were not somewhat darker
than Helen's—well, go to—there were no more
comparison between the women; but, for my part,          45
she is my kinswoman: I would not, as they term it,
praise her, but I would somebody had heard her
talk yesterday, as I did. I will not dispraise your
sister Cassandra's wit, but——

TROILUS. O Pandarus! I tell thee, Pandarus,          50
When I do tell thee, there my hopes lie drowned,
Reply not in how many fathoms deep
They lie indrenched. I tell thee I am mad
In Cressid's love; thou answer'st she is fair,
Pour'st in the open ulcer of my heart          55
Her eyes, her hair, her cheek, her gait, her voice;
(Handlest in thy discourse, O, that her hand
In whose comparison all whites are ink,
Writing their own reproach; to whose soft seizure
The cygnet's down is harsh, and spirit of sense          60
Hard as the palm of plowman. This thou tell'st me,

---

30 *blench* flinch   37 *rive* split   39 *a-scorn* grudgingly   43 *An* if;
used throughout the play   57 *that her hand* that hand of hers   60
*cygnet's* young swan's   60 *sense* i.e., of touch

As true thou tell'st me, when I say I love her;
But, saying)* thus, instead of oil and balm,
Thou lay'st in every gash that love hath given me
The knife that made it.                                   65

PANDARUS. I speak no more than truth.

TROILUS. Thou dost not speak so much.

PANDARUS. Faith, I'll not meddle in it; let her be as
she is. If she be fair, 'tis the better for her; and she
be not, she has the mends in her own hands.              70

TROILUS. Good Pandarus, how now, Pandarus?

PANDARUS. I have had my labor for my travail; ill
thought on of her, and ill thought of you; gone between and between, but small thanks for my labor.

TROILUS. What, art thou angry, Pandarus? What, with   75
me?

PANDARUS. Because she's kin to me, therefore she's
not so fair as Helen. An she were not kin to me,
she would be as fair a' Friday as Helen is on Sunday. But what care I? I care not an she were a      80
blackamoor; 'tis all one to me.

TROILUS. Say I she is not fair?

PANDARUS. I do not care whether you do or no. She's
a fool to stay behind her father. Let her to the
Greeks, and so I'll tell her the next time I see her.   85
For my part, I'll meddle nor make no more i' th'
matter.

TROILUS. Pandarus——

PANDARUS. Not I.

TROILUS. Sweet Pandarus——                              90

PANDARUS. Pray you, speak no more to me. I will leave
all as I found it, and there an end.

                              *Exit. Sound alarum.*

TROILUS. Peace, you ungracious clamors! Peace, rude
sounds!

70 *mends* remedies, i.e., cosmetics    72 *travail* labor, also pun on
travel    79–80 *as fair . . . on Sunday* as fair in weekday clothes as
Helen in her Sunday best    84 *father* Calchas, a seer, who was fore-
warned by Apollo of the Trojan defeat and deserted to the Greeks
93s.d. *Alarum* signal "to arms"

Fools on both sides! Helen must needs be fair,
When with your blood you daily paint her thus.          9⁵
I cannot fight upon this argument;
It is too starved a subject for my sword.
But Pandarus—O gods, how do you plague me!
I cannot come to Cressid but by Pandar;
And he's as tetchy to be wooed to woo          10⁰
As she is stubborn, chaste, against all suit.
Tell me, Apollo, for thy Daphne's love,
What Cressid is, what Pandar, and what we.
Her bed is India; there she lies, a pearl.
Between our Ilium and where she resides          10⁵
Let it be called the wild and wand'ring flood,
Ourself the merchant, and this sailing Pandar
Our doubtful hope, our convoy and our bark.

*Alarum. Enter Aeneas.**

AENEAS. How now, Prince Troilus, wherefore not
     afield?
TROILUS. Because not there. This woman's answer
     sorts,          11⁰
For womanish it is to be from thence.
What news, Aeneas, from the field today?
AENEAS. That Paris is returnèd home, and hurt.
TROILUS. By whom, Aeneas?
AENEAS.                    Troilus, by Menelaus.
TROILUS. Let Paris bleed; 'tis but a scar to scorn:          11⁵
     Paris is gored with Menelaus' horn.          *Alarum.*
AENEAS. Hark what good sport is out of town today!
TROILUS. Better at home, if "would I might" were
     "may."
But to the sport abroad; are you bound thither?
AENEAS. In all swift haste.
TROILUS.                    Come, go we then together.          12⁰
                                        *Exeunt.*

96 *argument* subject, i.e., Helen's beauty   100 *tetchy* peevish   102
*Daphne* nymph who fled Apollo's love   105 *Ilium* Priam's palace
in this play   110 *sorts* fits   116 *horn* symbol of a cuckold

### ⋇§ I . ii §⋇

[*Troy. A street.*]

*Enter Cressida and [Alexander,] her man.*

CRESSIDA. Who were those went by?

MAN.                    Queen Hecuba and Helen.

CRESSIDA. And whither go they?

MAN.                        Up to the eastern tower,
  (Whose height commands as subject all the vale,)
  To see the battle. Hector, whose patience
  Is as a virtue fixed, today was moved.                    5
  He chid Andromache, and struck his armorer,
  (And, like as there were husbandry in war,
  Before the sun rose he was harnessed light,)
  And to the field goes he, where every flower
  Did, as a prophet, weep what it foresaw              10
  In Hector's wrath.

CRESSIDA.              What was his cause of anger?

MAN. The noise goes, this: there is among the Greeks
  A lord of Troyan blood, nephew to Hector;
  They call him Ajax.

CRESSIDA.          Good; and what of him?

MAN. They say he is a very man per se                    15
  And stands alone.

CRESSIDA. So do all men unless they are drunk, sick,
  or have no legs.

(MAN. This man, lady, hath robbed many beasts of
  their particular additions. He is as valiant as the      20
  lion, churlish as the bear, slow as the elephant; a
  man into whom nature hath so crowded humors

I.ii.5 *moved* impassioned    7 *husbandry* good domestic management
8 *harnessed* armored    20 *additions* epithets added to a man's name
to indicate rank or distinction    22 *humors* bodily fluids, the proper
balance of which yielded health, but the excess of one which led to
emotional disturbance

that his valor is crushed into folly, his folly sauced
with discretion. There is no man hath a virtue that
he hath not a glimpse of, nor any man an attaint          25
but he carries some stain of it. He is melancholy
without cause and merry against the hair. He hath
the joints of everything, but everything so out of
joint that he is a gouty Briareus, many hands and
no use, or purblind Argus, all eyes and no sight.          30

CRESSIDA. But how should this man that makes me
smile make Hector angry?)

MAN. They say he yesterday coped Hector in the
battle and struck him down, the disdain and shame
whereof hath ever since kept Hector fasting and          35
waking.

*Enter Pandarus.*

CRESSIDA. Who comes here?

MAN. Madam, your uncle Pandarus.

CRESSIDA. Hector's a gallant man.

MAN. As may be in the world, lady.          40

PANDARUS. What's that? What's that?

CRESSIDA. Good morrow, uncle Pandarus.

PANDARUS. Good morrow, cousin Cressid. What do
you talk of? Good morrow, Alexander. How do
you, cousin? When were you at Ilium?          45

CRESSIDA. This morning, uncle.

PANDARUS. What were you talking of when I came?
Was Hector armed and gone ere ye came to Ilium?
Helen was not up, was she?

CRESSIDA. Hector was gone, but Helen was not up.          50

PANDARUS. E'en so, Hector was stirring early.

CRESSIDA. That were we talking of, and of his anger.

PANDARUS. Was he angry?

CRESSIDA. So he says here.

25 *glimpse* spark   25 *attaint* blemish on honor   27 *hair* natural
tendency   29 *Briareus* a hundred-handed monster   30 *Argus* a
herdsman with eyes over his entire body   33 *coped* fought with
43 *cousin* used loosely; here, niece

PANDARUS. True, he was so; I know the cause too. 55
He'll lay about him today, I can tell them that;
and there's Troilus will not come far behind him.
Let them take heed of Troilus, I can tell them that
too.

CRESSIDA. What, is he angry too? 60

PANDARUS. Who, Troilus? Troilus is the better man of
the two.

CRESSIDA. O Jupiter! There's no comparison.

PANDARUS. What, not between Troilus and Hector? Do
you know a man if you see him? 65

CRESSIDA. Ay, if I ever saw him before and knew him.

PANDARUS. Well, I say Troilus is Troilus.

CRESSIDA. Then you say as I say, for I am sure he is
not Hector.

PANDARUS. No, nor Hector is not Troilus in some de- 70
grees.

CRESSIDA. 'Tis just to each of them; he is himself.

PANDARUS. Himself? Alas, poor Troilus, I would he
were.

CRESSIDA. So he is. 75

(PANDARUS. Condition, I had gone barefoot to India.

CRESSIDA. He is not Hector.)

PANDARUS. Himself? No, he's not himself. Would 'a
were himself. Well, the gods are above; time must
friend or end. Well Troilus, well, I would my heart 80
were in her body. No, Hector is not a better man
than Troilus.

CRESSIDA. Excuse me.

PANDARUS. He is elder.

CRESSIDA. Pardon me, pardon me. 85

PANDARUS. Th' other's not come to't; you shall tell me
another tale when th' other's come to't. Hector shall
not have his will this year.

CRESSIDA. He shall not need it if he have his own.

70–71 in some degrees by a long sight   76 Condition . . . India For
that result I'd go barefoot to India   78 'a he, used throughout the
play   86 come to't come to manhood

PANDARUS. Nor his qualities.                                    90

CRESSIDA. No matter.

PANDARUS. Nor his beauty.

CRESSIDA. 'Twould not become him. His own's better.

PANDARUS. You have no judgment, niece. (Helen herself swore th' other day that Troilus, for a brown       95
favor—for so 'tis, I must confess—not brown
neither——

CRESSIDA. No, but brown.

PANDARUS. Faith, to say truth, brown and not brown.

CRESSIDA. To say the truth, true and not true.          100

PANDARUS. She praised his complexion above Paris.

CRESSIDA. Why, Paris hath color enough.

PANDARUS. So he has.

CRESSIDA. Then Troilus should have too much. If she
praised him above, his complexion is higher than        105
his. He having color enough, and the other higher,
is too flaming a praise for a good complexion. I had
as lief Helen's golden tongue had commended
Troilus for a copper nose.)

PANDARUS. I swear to you, I think Helen loves him*      110
better than Paris.

CRESSIDA. Then she's a merry Greek indeed.

PANDARUS. Nay, I am sure she does. She came to him
th' other day into the compassed window—and,
you know, he has not past three or four hairs on his    115
chin——

CRESSIDA. Indeed, a tapster's arithmetic may soon
bring his particulars therein to a total.

PANDARUS. Why, he is very young; and yet will he,
within three pound, lift as much as his brother         120
Hector.

CRESSIDA. Is he so young a man, and so old a lifter?

PANDARUS. But to prove to you that Helen loves him,
she came and puts me her white hand to his cloven
chin——                                                  125

95–96 *brown favor* dark complexion     112 *a merry Greek* i.e., lighthearted and wanton     114 *compassed* bay     122 *so old a lifter* so
experienced a thief

CRESSIDA. Juno have mercy; how came it cloven?

PANDARUS. Why, you know 'tis dimpled; I think his smiling becomes him better than any man in all Phrygia.

CRESSIDA. O, he smiles valiantly.    130

PANDARUS. Does he not?

CRESSIDA. O, yes, an 'twere a cloud in autumn.

PANDARUS. Why, go to then. But to prove to you that Helen loves Troilus——

CRESSIDA. Troilus will stand to the proof if you'll    135 prove it so.

PANDARUS. Troilus? Why, he esteems her no more than I esteem an addle egg.

CRESSIDA. If you love an addle egg as well as you love an idle head, you would eat chickens i' the shell.    140

PANDARUS. I cannot choose but laugh to think how she tickled his chin. Indeed, she has a marvel's white hand, I must needs confess.

CRESSIDA. Without the rack.

PANDARUS. And she takes upon her to spy a white hair    145 on his chin.

CRESSIDA. Alas poor chin, many a wart is richer.

PANDARUS. But there was such laughing. Queen Hecuba laughed that her eyes ran o'er.

CRESSIDA. With millstones.    150

PANDARUS. And Cassandra laughed.

CRESSIDA. But there was a more temperate fire under the pot of her eyes. Did her eyes run o'er too?

PANDARUS. And Hector laughed.

CRESSIDA. At what was all this laughing?    155

PANDARUS. Marry, at the white hair that Helen spied on Troilus' chin.

CRESSIDA. An't had been a green hair, I should have laughed too.

PANDARUS. They laughed not so much at the hair as at    160 his pretty answer.

CRESSIDA. What was his answer?

138 *addle* rotten    144 *rack* torture    156 *Marry* contracted version of the oath "By the Virgin Mary," used throughout the play

PANDARUS. Quoth she, "Here's but two-and-fifty hairs
on your chin, and one of them is white."

CRESSIDA. This is her question.     165

PANDARUS. That's true, make no question of that.
"Two-and-fifty hairs," quoth he, "and one white.
That white hair is my father, and all the rest are
his sons." "Jupiter!" quoth she, "which of these
hairs is Paris, my husband?" "The forked one,"     170
quoth he; "pluck't out, and give it him." But there
was such laughing, and Helen so blushed, and
Paris so chafed, and all the rest so laughed, that
it passed.

CRESSIDA. So let it now, for it has been a great while     175
going by.

PANDARUS. Well, cousin, I told you a thing yesterday;
think on't.

CRESSIDA. So I do.

PANDARUS. I'll be sworn 'tis true; he will weep you,     180
an 'twere a man born in April.     *Sound a retreat.*

CRESSIDA. And I'll spring up in his tears, an 'twere a
nettle against May.*

PANDARUS. Hark, they are coming from the field. Shall
we stand up here and see them as they pass toward     185
Ilium? Good niece, do; sweet niece, Cressida.

CRESSIDA. At your pleasure.

PANDARUS. Here, here, here's an excellent place; here
we may see most bravely. I'll tell you them all by
their names as they pass by, but mark Troilus above     190
the rest.

*Enter Aeneas [and passes across the stage].*

CRESSIDA. Speak not so loud.

PANDARUS. That's Aeneas. Is not that a brave man?
He's one of the flowers of Troy, I can tell you. But
mark Troilus; you shall see anon.     195

171 *give it him* i.e., the forked hair resembling cuckold's horns
174 *passed* exceeded all bounds     181 *an* as if     183 *against* in expectation of     189 *bravely* excellently

*Enter Antenor [and passes across the stage].*

CRESSIDA. Who's that?

PANDARUS. That's Antenor. He has a shrewd wit, I can
  tell you; and he's man good enough—he's one o'
  the soundest judgments in Troy whosoever, and a
  proper man of person. When comes Troilus? I'll     200
  show you Troilus anon. If he see me, you shall see
  him nod at me.

(CRESSIDA. Will he give you the nod?)

PANDARUS. You shall see.

(CRESSIDA. If he do, the rich shall have more.)     205

*Enter Hector [and passes across the stage].*

PANDARUS. That's Hector, that, that, look you, that;
  there's a fellow! Go thy way, Hector! There's a
  brave man, niece. O brave Hector! Look how he
  looks; there's a countenance! Is't not a brave man?

CRESSIDA. O, a brave man.     210

PANDARUS. Is 'a not? It does a man's heart good. Look
  you what hacks are on his helmet. Look you yonder, do you see? Look you there. There's no jesting;
  there's laying on, take't off who will, as they say.
  There be hacks!     215

CRESSIDA. Be those with swords?

PANDARUS. Swords, anything, he cares not; an the
  devil come to him, it's all one. By God's lid, it
  does one's heart good.

*Enter Paris [and passes across the stage].*

Yonder comes Paris, yonder comes Paris. Look ye     220
  yonder, niece. Is't not a gallant man too, is't not?
  Why, this is brave now. Who said he came hurt
  home today? He's not hurt. Why, this will do

---

200 *proper man of person* handsome man in figure     203 *nod* play
on 'noddy,' simpleton     205 *the rich shall have more* the one rich
in foolishness, i.e., Pandar, will receive even more foolishness     214
*laying on* i.e., of blows     221 *gallant* general term of praise

Helen's heart good now, ha? Would I could see
Troilus now. You shall see Troilus anon.                    225
CRESSIDA. Who's that?

*Enter Helenus [and passes across the stage].*

PANDARUS. That's Helenus. I marvel where Troilus is.
That's Helenus. I think he went not forth today.
That's Helenus.
CRESSIDA. Can Helenus fight, uncle?                          230
PANDARUS. Helenus? No. Yes, he'll fight indifferent
well. I marvel where Troilus is. Hark, do you not
hear the people cry "Troilus"? Helenus is a priest.
CRESSIDA. What sneaking fellow comes yonder?

*Enter Troilus [and passes across the stage].*

PANDARUS. Where? Yonder? That's Deiphobus. 'Tis            235
Troilus! There's a man, niece, hem? Brave Troilus,
the prince of chivalry!
CRESSIDA. Peace, for shame, peace!
PANDARUS. Mark him, note him. O brave Troilus!
Look well upon him, niece. Look you how his           240
sword is bloodied, and his helm more hacked than
Hector's—and how he looks, and how he goes. O
admirable youth! He never saw three-and-twenty.
Go thy way, Troilus, go thy way! Had I a sister
were a grace, or a daughter a goddess, he should      245
take his choice. O admirable man! Paris? Paris is
dirt to him; and I warrant Helen, to change, would
give an eye to boot.

*Enter Common Soldiers.*

CRESSIDA. Here comes more.
PANDARUS. Asses, fools, dolts; chaff and bran, chaff       250
and bran; porridge after meat. I could live and die
in the eyes of Troilus. Ne'er look, ne'er look. The
eagles are gone; crows and daws, crows and daws.
I had rather be such a man as Troilus than Agamemnon and all Greece.                                       255

245 *grace* attendant goddess

CRESSIDA. There is amongst the Greeks Achilles, a better man than Troilus.

PANDARUS. Achilles? A drayman, a porter, a very camel.

CRESSIDA. Well, well.   260

PANDARUS. "Well, well"? Why, have you any discretion, have you any eyes, do you know what a man is? Is not birth, beauty, good shape, discourse, manhood, learning, gentleness, virtue, youth, liberality, and such like, the spice and salt that season   265
a man?

CRESSIDA. Ay, a minced man; (and then to be baked with no date in the pie, for then the man's date is out.)

PANDARUS. You are such a woman a man knows not   270
at what ward you lie.

CRESSIDA. Upon my back, to defend my belly; upon my wit, to defend my wiles; upon my secrecy, to defend mine honesty; my mask, to defend my beauty; and you, to defend all these. And at all these   275
wards I lie, at a thousand watches.

PANDARUS. Say one of your watches.

CRESSIDA. Nay, I'll watch you for that; and that's one of the chiefest of them too. If I cannot ward what I would not have hit, I can watch you for telling   280
how I took the blow; unless it swell past hiding, and then it's past watching.

PANDARUS. You are such another!

*Enter [Troilus'] Boy.*

BOY. Sir, my lord would instantly speak with you.

PANDARUS. Where?   285

BOY. At your own house. There he unarms him.

PANDARUS. Good boy, tell him I come.   [*Exit Boy.*]
I doubt he be hurt. Fare ye well, good niece.

CRESSIDA. Adieu, uncle.

267 *minced* (1) chopped into bits (2) affected   271 *ward* posture of defense in swordplay   274 *honesty* chastity   276 *watches* periods of the night

PANDARUS. I will be with you, niece, by and by.          290
CRESSIDA. To bring, uncle.
PANDARUS. Ay, a token from Troilus.
CRESSIDA. By the same token, you are a bawd.

                                        *Exit Pandarus.*

Words, vows, gifts, tears, and love's full sacrifice
He offers in another's enterprise;          295
But more in Troilus thousandfold I see
Than in the glass of Pandar's praise may be.
Yet hold I off. Women are angels, wooing;
Things won are done, joy's soul lies in the doing.
That she beloved knows nought that knows not          300
  this:
Men prize the thing ungained more than it is;
That she was never yet, that ever knew
Love got so sweet as when desire did sue.
Therefore this maxim out of love I teach:
Achievement is command; ungained, beseech.          305
Then, though my heart's content firm love doth
  bear,
Nothing of that shall from mine eyes appear.     *Exit.*


               ᪲ I. iii ᪲

[*The Greek camp, Before Agamemnon's pavilion.*]*


     *Sennet. Enter Agamemnon, Nestor, Ulysses, Dio-
          medes, Menelaus, with others.*

AGAMEMNON. Princes,
    What grief hath set the jaundice on your cheeks?
    The ample proposition that hope makes

290–91 *be with you . . . To bring* a cant expression apparently
meaning "get even with you" or, in reference to women, "overcome" in a lascivious sense; Cressida mocks Pandarus's innocent
farewell    298 *wooing* while being wooed    301 *it is* its value
303 *got* i.e., by men    305 *Achievement . . . beseech* having
achieved love, men command; before love is gained, they plead
I.iii.s.d. *Sennet* a trumpet call indicating a procession

In all designs begun on earth below
Fails in the promised largeness. Checks and disas-    5
ters
Grow in the veins of actions highest reared,
As knots, by the conflux of meeting sap,
Infects the sound pine and diverts his grain
Tortive and errant from his course of growth.
Nor, princes, is it matter new to us    10
That we come short of our suppose so far
That after seven years' siege yet Troy walls stand;
Sith every action that hath gone before,
Whereof we have record, trial did draw
Bias and thwart, not answering the aim    15
And that unbodied figure of the thought
That gave't surmisèd shape. Why then, you princes,
Do you with cheeks abashed behold our works
And call them shames, which are indeed nought
else
But the protractive trials of great Jove    20
To find persistive constancy in men?
(The fineness of which metal is not found
In Fortune's love; for then, the bold and coward,
The wise and fool, the artist and unread,
The hard and soft, seem all affined and kin.    25
But, in the wind and tempest of her frown,
Distinction, with a broad and powerful fan,
Puffing at all, winnows the light away,
And what hath mass or matter by itself
Lies rich in virtue and unmingled.)    30
NESTOR. With due observance of thy godlike seat,
Great Agamemnon, Nestor shall apply
Thy latest words. In the reproof of chance
Lies the true proof of men. The sea being smooth,
How many shallow bauble boats dare sail    35
Upon her patient breast, making their way

7 *conflux* flowing together    9 *Tortive and errant* distorted and wan-
dering    11 *suppose* expectation    15 *Bias and thwart* to one side
and crosswise    24 *artist* learned    25 *affined* closely related    30
*unmingled* unmixed with poor substance

With those of nobler bulk?
But let the ruffian Boreas once enrage
The gentle Thetis, (and anon behold
The strong-ribbed bark through liquid mountains     40
  cut,
Bounding between the two moist elements
Like Perseus' horse,) where's then the saucy boat,
Whose weak untimbered sides but even now
Corrivaled greatness? Either to harbor fled,
Or made a toast for Neptune. Even so     45
Doth valor's show and valor's worth divide
In storms of fortune. (For in her ray and brightness
The herd hath more annoyance by the breese
Than by the tiger; but when the splitting wind
Makes flexible the knees of knotted oaks,     50
And flies fled under shade, why then the thing of
  courage,
As roused with rage, with rage doth sympathize,
And with an accent tuned in selfsame key
Returns to chiding fortune.)
ULYSSES.                              Agamemnon,
  Thou great commander, nerves and bone of     55
  Greece,
(Heart of our numbers, soul and only spirit,
In whom the tempers and the minds of all
Should be shut up, hear what Ulysses speaks.
Besides th' applause and approbation
The which [to Agamemnon], most mighty for thy     60
  place and sway,)
[to Nestor] And thou most reverend* (for thy
  stretched-out life,
I give to both your speeches—which were such
As Agamemnon and the hand of Greece

38 *Boreas* north wind     39 *Thetis* a sea maiden, Achilles' mother,
but here the sea     42 *Perseus' horse* Pegasus, the winged horse     45
*toast* piece of toast soaked in wine     46 *show* appearance     48
*breese* gadfly     54 *Returns* replies     55 *nerves* sinews     58 *shut up*
gathered in

Should hold up high in brass; and such again
As venerable Nestor, hatched in silver,                    65
Should with a bond of air, strong as the axletree
On which heaven rides, knit all the Greekish ears
To his experienced tongue—yet let it please both,
Thou great, and wise, to) hear Ulysses speak.

AGAMEMNON. Speak, Prince of Ithaca; (and be't of less    70
    expect
That matter needless, of importless burden,
Divide thy lips than we are confident,
When rank Thersites opes his mastic jaws,
We shall hear music, wit, and oracle.)

ULYSSES. Troy, yet upon his basis, had been down,'        75
And the great Hector's sword had lacked a master,
But for these instances.
The specialty of rule hath been neglected;
And look, how many Grecian tents do stand
Hollow upon this plain, so many hollow factions.         80
When that the general is not like the hive
To whom the foragers shall all repair,
What honey is expected? Degree being vizarded,
Th' unworthiest shows as fairly in the mask.
The heavens themselves, the planets, and this center     85
Observe degree, priority, and place,
(Insisture, course, proportion, season, form,)
Office, and custom, in all line of order.
(And therefore is the glorious planet Sol
In noble eminence enthroned and sphered                   90
Amidst the other; whose med'cinable eye

65 *hatched in silver* with silver lines in his hair    73 *mastic* abusive
77 *instances* causes    78 *The speciality of rule* the particular rights
of supreme authority    81–83 *When . . . expected* whenever the
general (social good? commander?) is not like a hive to whom the
foragers, i.e. the soldiers, shall all repair (return? relate?)    83 *Degree being vizarded* the heierarchy of authority being hidden    85
*center* earth in Ptolemaic system    87 *Insisture* constancy of position
89 *Sol* sun, considered a planet in Ptolemaic system    91 *other*
others

Corrects the influence of evil planets,
And posts, like the commandment of a king,
Sans check, to good and bad.) But when the planets
In evil mixture to disorder wander,                          95
(What plagues, and what portents, what mutiny,)
What raging of the sea, shaking of earth,
Commotion in the winds, frights, changes, horrors,
Divert and crack, rend and deracinate
The unity and married calm of states                        100
Quite from their fixure? O, when degree is shaked,
Which is the ladder of all high designs,
The enterprise is sick. (How could communities,
Degrees in schools, and brotherhoods in cities,
Peaceful commerce from dividable shores,                    105
The primogenity and due of birth,
Prerogative of age, crowns, scepters, laurels,
But by degree, stand in authentic place?)
Take but degree away, untune that string,
And hark what discord follows. (Each thing meets   110
In mere oppugnancy.) The bounded waters
Should lift their bosoms higher than the shores
And make a sop of all this solid globe;
Strength should be lord of imbecility,
And the rude son should strike his father dead;            115
(Force should be right, or rather right and wrong—
Between whose endless jar justice resides—
Should lose their names, and so should justice too.)
Then everything include itself in power,
Power into will, will into appetite,                        120
And appetite, an universal wolf,
(So doubly seconded with will and power,)
Must make perforce an universal prey
And last eat up himself. Great Agamemnon,

92 *influence* astrological effect   99 *deracinate* uproot   106 *primogenity* right of eldest son to succeed to father's estate   111 *mere
oppugnancy* total strife   114 *imbecility* i.e., physical weakness   117
*jar* discordant clash   119 *include itself in power* convert itself into
power

This chaos, when degree is suffocate,                    125
Follows the choking.
And this neglection of degree (it is
That by a pace goes backward with a purpose
It hath to climb. The general's disdained
By him one step below, he by the next,              130
That next by him beneath; so every step,)
Exampled by the first pace that is sick
Of his superior, grows to an envious fever
(Of pale and bloodless emulation;)
And 'tis this fever that keeps Troy on foot,         135
Not her own sinews. To end a tale of length,
Troy in our weakness stands, not in her strength.
NESTOR. Most wisely hath Ulysses here discovered
The fever whereof all our power is sick.
AGAMEMNON. The nature of the sickness found,
     Ulysses,                                          140
What is the remedy?
ULYSSES. The great Achilles, whom opinion crowns
The sinew and the forehand of our host,
Having his ear full of his airy fame,
Grows dainty of his worth, and in his tent        145
Lies mocking our designs. With him Patroclus
Upon a lazy bed the livelong day
Breaks scurril jests,
And with ridiculous and silly action,
Which, slanderer, he imitation calls,                150
He pageants us. (Sometime, great Agamemnon,
Thy topless deputation he puts on,
And, like a strutting player, whose conceit
Lies in his hamstring, and doth think it rich

---

127–29 And this neglection . . . climb this neglect of heierarchy
affects succeeding subordinates when it (the pace? neglect?) attempts to climb above the next in rank    143 forehand mainstay
145 dainty of fastidious about    151 pageants mimics    152 topless
deputation supreme authority    153–54 conceit Lies in his hamstring imagination rests in the tendon at the back of his knee, i.e.,
his bowing

To hear the wooden dialogue and sound,                    155
'Twixt his stretched footing and the scaffoldage,
Such to-be-pitied and o'erwrested seeming
He acts thy greatness in.) And when he speaks,
'Tis like a chime a-mending, (with terms un-
    squared,
Which, from the tongue of roaring Typhon drop-
    ped,                                                   160
Would seem hyperboles.) At this fusty stuff
The large Achilles, on his pressed bed lolling,
From his deep chest laughs out a loud applause,
Cries, "Excellent! 'tis Agamemnon right.
Now play me Nestor; hem, and stroke thy beard,           165
(As he being drest to some oration."
That's done as near as the extremest ends
Of parallels, as like as Vulcan and his wife,
Yet god Achilles still cries, "Excellent!
'Tis Nestor right. Now play him me, Patroclus,           170
Arming to answer in a night alarm."
And then, forsooth, the faint defects of age
Must be the scene of mirth; to cough and spit,
And with a palsy fumbling on his gorget,
Shake in and out the rivet. And at this sport            175
Sir Valor dies; cries, "O, enough, Patroclus,
Or give me ribs of steel; I shall split all
In pleasure of my spleen!") And in this fashion
All our abilities, gifts,* (natures, shapes,
Severals and generals of grace exact,                    180
Achievements, plots, orders, preventions,)
Excitements to the field or speech for truce,
(Success or loss, what is or is not, serves)

156 *stretched footing* exaggerated strides    156 *scaffoldage* stage
157 *o'erwrested seeming* strained imitation    159 *unsquared* distorted    160 *Typhon* a serpent-headed monster with a thundering
voice    161 *fusty* stale    168 V*ulcan and his wife* Vulcan, god of
the forge, was lame; his wife was Venus    174 *gorget* throat armor
178 *spleen* considered the seat of emotions, here of hilarity    180
*Severals and generals* individual and common

As stuff for these two to make paradoxes.
NESTOR. And in the imitation of these twain,                    185
   Who, as Ulysses says, opinion crowns
   With an imperial voice, many are infect.
   Ajax is grown self-willed, and bears his head
   In such a rein, in full as proud a place
   As broad Achilles; keeps his tent like him;          190
   Makes factious feasts; rails on our state of war,
   Bold as an oracle, and sets Thersites,
   A slave whose gall coins slanders like a mint,
   To match us in comparisons with dirt,
   To weaken and discredit our exposure,               195
   How rank soever rounded in with danger.
ULYSSES. They tax our policy and call it cowardice,
   Count wisdom as no member of the war,
   (Forestall prescience,) and esteem no act
   But that of hand. The still and mental parts         200
   That do contrive how many hands shall strike
   When fitness calls them on, and know by measure
   Of their observant toil the enemies' weight—
   Why, this hath not a finger's dignity.
   They call this bed-work, mapp'ry, closet war;        205
   (So that the ram that batters down the wall,
   For the great swinge and rudeness of his poise,
   They place before his hand that made the engine,
   Or those that with the fineness of their souls
   By reason guide his execution.)                      210
NESTOR. Let this be granted, and Achilles' horse
   Makes many Thetis' sons.                *Tucket.*
AGAMEMNON. What trumpet? Look, Menelaus.
MENELAUS. From Troy.

---

184 *paradoxes* mockeries, possibly parodies    189 *In such a rein* i.e.,
so haughtily    190 *broad* arrogant    193 *gall* source of bile, hence
producer of bitterness and rancor    196 *rank* densely    197 *tax*
criticize    199 *Forestall prescience* discount foresight    205 *mapp'ry*
map work    207 *swinge* impetus    207 *poise* weight    211 *Achilles'
horse* his horsemen, the Myrmidons    212s.d. *Tucket* fanfare on a
trumpet

*Enter Aeneas.**

AGAMEMNON. What would you 'fore our tent?                    215

AENEAS. Is this great Agamemnon's tent, I pray you?

AGAMEMNON. Even this.

AENEAS. May one that is a herald and a prince
  Do a fair message to his kingly eyes?

AGAMEMNON. With surety stronger than Achilles' arm          220
  'Fore all the Greekish heads, which with one voice
  Call Agamemnon head and general.

AENEAS. Fair leave and large security. How may
  A stranger to those most imperial looks
  Know them from eyes of other mortals?

AGAMEMNON.                                    How?          225

AENEAS. Ay.
  I ask, that I might waken reverence,
  And bid the cheek be ready with a blush
  Modest as morning when she coldly eyes
  The youthful Phoebus.                                      230
  Which is that god in office, guiding men?
  Which is the high and mighty Agamemnon?

AGAMEMNON. This Troyan scorns us, or the men of
    Troy
  Are ceremonious courtiers.

AENEAS. Courtiers as free, as debonair, unarmed,            235
  As bending angels; that's their fame in peace.
  But when they would seem soldiers, they have galls,
  Good arms, strong joints, true swords—and, great
    Jove's accord,
  Nothing so full of heart. (But peace, Aeneas;
  Peace, Troyan; lay thy finger on thy lips.                240
  The worthiness of praise distains his worth,
  If that the praised himself bring the praise forth.
  But what the repining enemy commends,
  That breath fame blows; that praise, sole pure,
    transcends.)

230 *Phoebus* Phoebus Apollo, the sun god   236 *bending* bowing
238 *Jove's accord* i.e., if Jove be on their side   241 *distains* sullies

AGAMEMNON. Sir, you of Troy, call you yourself
    Aeneas?                                                                                 245
AENEAS. Ay, Greek, that is my name.
AGAMEMNON. What's your affair, I pray you?
AENEAS. Sir, pardon; 'tis for Agamemnon's ears.
AGAMEMNON. He hears nought privately that comes
    from Troy.
AENEAS. Nor I from Troy come not to whisper him.    250
    I bring a trumpet to awake his ear,
    To set his seat on the attentive bent,
    And then to speak.
AGAMEMNON.        Speak frankly as the wind;
    It is not Agamemnon's sleeping hour.
    That thou shalt know, Troyan, he is awake,                          255
    He tells thee so himself.
AENEAS.            Trumpet, blow loud,
    Send thy brass voice through all these lazy tents;
    And every Greek of mettle, let him know,
    What Troy means fairly shall be spoke aloud.
                           *Sound trumpet.*
    We have, great Agamemnon, here in Troy                             260
    A prince called Hector—Priam is his father—
    Who in this dull and long-continued truce
    Is rusty grown. He bade me take a trumpet,
    And to this purpose speak: kings, princes, lords,
    If there be one among the fair'st of Greece  ·                      265
    That holds his honor higher than his ease,
    That seeks his praise more than he fears his peril,
    That knows his valor and knows not his fear,
    That loves his mistress more than in confession
    With truant vows to her own lips he loves,                          270
    And dare avow her beauty and her worth
    In other arms than hers—to him this challenge;
    Hector, in view of Troyans and of Greeks,
    Shall make it good, or do his best to do it;

252 *To . . . bent* to alert his place of authority to pay attention
269–70 *more than . . . lips he loves* more than he asserts with false
oaths directly to her face

He hath a lady wiser, fairer, truer,                        275
Than ever Greek did compass in his arms;
And will tomorrow with his trumpet call,
Midway between your tents and walls of Troy,
To rouse a Grecian that is true in love.
If any come, Hector shall honor him;                        280
If none, he'll say in Troy when he retires,
The Grecian dames are sunburnt and not worth
The splinter of a lance. Even so much.

AGAMEMNON. This shall be told our lovers, Lord
    Aeneas;
If none of them have soul in such a kind,                   285
We left them all at home. But we are soldiers;
And may that soldier a mere recreant prove,
That means not, hath not, or is not in love!
If then one is, or hath, or means to be,
That one meets Hector; if none else, I am he.              290

NESTOR. Tell him of Nestor, one that was a man
When Hector's grandsire sucked. He is old now,
But if there be not in our Grecian host
A nobleman that hath one spark of fire
To answer for his love, tell him from me,                  295
I'll hide my silver beard in a gold beaver,
And in my vantbrace put my withered brawns,
And, meeting him, will tell him that my lady
Was fairer than his grandam, and as chaste
As may be in the world. His youth in flood,                300
I'll prove this truth with my three drops of blood.

AENEAS. Now heavens forfend such scarcity of youth!

ULYSSES. Amen.

AGAMEMNON. Fair Lord Aeneas, let me touch your
    hand;
To our pavilion shall I lead you first.                     305
Achilles shall have word of this intent;
So shall each lord of Greece, from tent to tent.

282 *sunburnt* sunburn was considered unattractive by the Eliza-
bethans   296 *beaver* face guard of a helmet   297 *vantbrace* pro-
tective armor for the forearm

Yourself shall feast with us before you go,
And find the welcome of a noble foe.

*Exeunt. Manent Ulysses and Nestor.*

ULYSSES. Nestor.                                             310
NESTOR. What says Ulysses?
ULYSSES. I have a young conception in my brain;
    Be you my time to bring it to some shape.
NESTOR. What is't?
(ULYSSES. This 'tis:                                         315
    Blunt wedges rive hard knots; the seeded pride
    That hath to this maturity blown up
    In rank Achilles, must or now be cropped
    Or, shedding, breed a nursery of like evil
    To overbulk us all.                                  320
NESTOR.                Well, and how?)
ULYSSES. This challenge that the gallant Hector sends,
    However it is spread in general name,
    Relates in purpose only to Achilles.
NESTOR. True, (the purpose is perspicuous as substance
    Whose grossness little characters sum up;)         325
    And, in the publication, make no strain
    But that Achilles, were his brain as barren
    As banks of Libya—though, Apollo knows,
    'Tis dry enough—will with great speed of judgment,
    Ay with celerity, find Hector's purpose            330
    Pointing on him.
ULYSSES. And wake him to the answer, think you?
NESTOR. Why, 'tis most meet. Who may you else op-
    pose
    That can from Hector bring his honor off,
    If not Achilles? Though't be a sportful combat,    335
    Yet in the trial much opinion dwells;

---

309s.d. *Manent . . . Nestor* Ulysses and Nestor remain    312 *young
conception* beginning of an idea    316–20 *seeded pride . . . us all*
sustained metaphor of a ripened pride that must be cut down, lest
by scattering its seeds it breed similar evil    326 *make no strain* you
can have no difficulty in believing    336 *opinion* reputation

For here the Troyans taste our dear'st repute
With their fin'st palate; and trust to me, Ulysses,
Our imputation shall be oddly poised
In this vild action. For the success,                          34❦
Although particular, shall give a scantling
Of good or bad unto the general;
(And in such indexes, although small pricks
To their subsequent volumes, there is seen
The baby figure of the giant mass                             34❦
Of things to come at large. It is supposed
He that meets Hector issues from our choice;
And choice, being mutual act of all our souls,
Makes merit her election, and doth boil,
As 'twere from forth us all, a man distilled                  35❦
Out of our virtues—who miscarrying,
What heart receives from hence a conquering part,
To steel a strong opinion to themselves;
Which entertained, limbs are his instruments,
In no less working than are swords and bows                   35❦
Directive by the limbs.)
ULYSSES. (Give pardon to my speech.) Therefore 'tis
    meet
    Achilles meet not Hector. Let us, like merchants,
    First show foul wares, and think perchance they'll
        sell;
    If not, the luster of the better shall exceed             36❦
    By showing the worst first. Do not consent
    That ever Hector and Achilles meet;
    For both our honor and our shame in this
    Are dogged with two strange followers.
NESTOR. I see them not with my old eyes; what are
    they?                                                      36❦

---

339–40 Our . . . action our reputation shall be precisely weighed in
this trivial action    341 scantling sample    342 general world at
large    343–44 small . . . volumes minor signs in comparison to
the succeeding weighty issues    349 election basis for choice    354
his i.e., of the strong opinion    364 followers consequences

ULYSSES. What glory our Achilles shares from Hector,
  Were he not proud, we all should share with him.
  But he already is too insolent,
  And it were better parch in Afric sun
  Than in the pride and salt scorn of his eyes,                370
  Should he 'scape Hector fair. If he were foiled,
  Why then we do our main opinion crush
  In taint of our best man. No, make a lott'ry;
  And by device let blockish Ajax draw
  The sort to fight with Hector. Among ourselves,          375
  Give him allowance for the better man,
  (For that will physic the great Myrmidon
  Who broils in loud applause, and make him fall
  His crest that prouder than blue Iris bends.)
  If the dull brainless Ajax comes safe off,                    380
  We'll dress him up in voices; if he fail,
  Yet go we under our opinion still
  That we have better men. But, hit or miss,
  Our project's life this shape of sense assumes:
  Ajax employed plucks down Achilles' plumes.            385
NESTOR. Now, Ulysses, I begin to relish thy advice,
  And I will give a taste thereof forthwith
  To Agamemnon. Go we to him straight.
  Two curs shall tame each other; pride alone
  Must tarre the mastiffs on, as 'twere a bone.              390
                                                   *Exeunt.*

370 *salt* bitter    372–73 *our main . . . man* the best of our reputation lose in the disgrace of our best fighter    375 *sort* lot    377
*physic* cure, purge    377 *the great Myrmidon* i.e., Achilles    378
*broils* i.e., suns himself    379 *Iris* the rainbow    390 *tarre* incite

### ᵕᔓ II. i ᔒᵛ

[*The Greek camp.*]


*Enter Ajax and Thersites.*

AJAX. Thersites!

THERSITES. Agamemnon, how if he had boils—full, all
over, generally?

AJAX. Thersites!

THERSITES. And those boils did run?—say so—did not        5
the general run then? Were not that a botchy core?

AJAX. Dog!

THERSITES. Then would come some matter from him.
I see none now.

AJAX. Thou bitch-wolf's son, canst thou not hear?        10
Feel then.        *Strikes him.*

THERSITES. The plague of Greece upon thee, thou
mongrel beef-witted lord!

✓ AJAX. Speak then, thou vinewed'st leaven, speak. I
will beat thee into handsomeness.        15

THERSITES. I shall sooner rail thee into wit and holi-
ness; but I think thy horse will sooner con an
oration than thou learn a prayer without book.
Thou canst strike, canst thou? A red murrain o'
thy jade's tricks!        20

J AJAX. Toadstool, learn me the proclamation.

THERSITES. Dost thou think I have no sense, thou
strikest me thus?

AJAX. The proclamation!

THERSITES. Thou art proclaimed fool, I think.        25

II.i.6 *botchy core* inflamed boil   14 *vinewed'st leaven* most mouldy
dough   17 *con* memorize   18 *without book* by heart   19 *murrain*
plague   20 *jade's* broken down horse's   21 *learn me* find out for
me

AJAX. Do not, porpentine, do not; my fingers itch.

THERSITES. I would thou didst itch from head to foot; an I had the scratching of thee, I would make thee the loathsomest scab in Greece. When thou art forth in the incursions, thou strikest as slow as another. 30

AJAX. I say, the proclamation!

THERSITES. Thou grumblest and railest every hour on Achilles, and thou art as full of envy at his greatness as Cerberus is at Proserpina's beauty, ay, that thou bark'st at him. 35

AJAX. Mistress Thersites!

THERSITES. Thou shouldst strike him.

AJAX. Cobloaf!

THERSITES. He would pun thee into shivers with his fist, as a sailor breaks a biscuit. 40

AJAX. You whoreson cur!     [Beating him.]

THERSITES. Do, do.

AJAX. Thou stool for a witch!

THERSITES. Ay, do, do, thou sodden-witted lord! thou hast no more brain than I have in mine elbows; an asinico may tutor thee. Thou scurvy-valiant ass, thou art here but to thrash Troyans, and thou art bought and sold among those of any wit like a barbarian slave. If thou use to beat me, I will begin at thy heel, and tell what thou art by inches, thou thing of no bowels, thou! 45 50

AJAX. You dog!

THERSITES. You scurvy lord!

AJAX. You cur!     [Beating him.] 55

THERSITES. Mars his idiot! Do, rudeness; do, camel; do, do.

---

26 *porpentine* porcupine   30 *incursions* attacks   35 *Cerberus* the three-headed watchdog of Hades   35 *Proserpina* the beautiful wife of Pluto   39 *Cobloaf* crusty, rounded loaf of bread   40 *pun* pound   44 *stool for a witch* fit only for a witch(?)   47 *asinico* young ass   49 *bought and sold* passed from one to another, i.e., made fun of   52 *bowels* mercy   56 *Mars his* Mars's

*Enter Achilles and Patroclus.*

ACHILLES. Why, how now, Ajax? wherefore do you
thus? How now, Thersites? what's the matter, man?

THERSITES. You see him there? Do you?                    60

ACHILLES. Ay, what's the matter?

THERSITES. Nay, look upon him.

ACHILLES. So I do. What's the matter?

THERSITES. Nay, but regard him well.

ACHILLES. "Well"—why so I do.                            65

THERSITES. But yet you look not well upon him; for,
whomsoever you take him to be, he is Ajax.

ACHILLES. I know that, fool.

THERSITES. Ay, but that fool knows not himself.

AJAX. Therefore I beat thee.                             70

THERSITES. Lo, lo, lo, lo, what modicums of wit he ut-
ters! His evasions have ears thus long. I have
bobbed his brain more than he has beat my bones.
I will buy nine sparrows for a penny, and his pia
mater is not worth the ninth part of a sparrow.       75
This lord, Achilles, Ajax, who wears his wit in his
belly and his guts in his head, I'll tell you what I
say of him.

ACHILLES. What?

THERSITES. I say, this Ajax——                           80
            [*Ajax attempts to strike him.*]

ACHILLES. Nay, good Ajax.

THERSITES. Has not so much wit——
            [*Ajax attempts again to strike him.*]

ACHILLES. Nay, I must hold you.

THERSITES. As will stop the eye of Helen's needle, for
whom he comes to fight.                               85

ACHILLES. Peace, fool!

THERSITES. I would have peace and quietness, but the
fool will not—he here, that he. Look you there.

69 *that fool* pretending Achilles has said "I know that fool"     72
*his evasions . . . long* his flights of fancy have ears as long as those
of an ass     73 *bobbed* pummeled     74–75 *pia mater* the membrane
covering the brain, here the brain itself

AJAX. O thou damned cur, I shall——

ACHILLES. Will you set your wit to a fool's?                    90

THERSITES. No, I warrant you; the fool's will shame it.

PATROCLUS. Good words, Thersites.

ACHILLES. What's the quarrel?

AJAX. I bade the vile owl go learn me the tenor of the
proclamation, and he rails upon me.                            95

THERSITES. I serve thee not.

AJAX. Well, go to, go to.

THERSITES. I serve here voluntary.

ACHILLES. Your last service was suff'rance, 'twas not
voluntary; no man is beaten voluntary. Ajax was           100
here the voluntary, and you as under an impress.

THERSITES. E'en so, a great deal of your wit, too, lies
in your sinews, or else there be liars. Hector shall
have a great catch if he knock out either of your
brains. 'A were as good crack a fusty nut with no         105
kernel.

ACHILLES. What, with me too, Thersites?

THERSITES. There's Ulysses and old Nestor, whose wit
was moldly ere your grandsires had nails on their
toes, yoke you like draft oxen and make you plow          110
up the wars.

ACHILLES. What, what?

THERSITES. Yes, good sooth. To, Achilles! To, Ajax!
To——                                                          115

AJAX. I shall cut out your tongue.

THERSITES. 'Tis no matter, I shall speak as much as
thou afterwards.

PATROCLUS. No more words, Thersites; peace!

THERSITES. I will hold my peace when Achilles' brach
bids me, shall I?                                             120

ACHILLES. There's for you, Patroclus.

THERSITES. I will see you hanged like clotpoles, ere

90 *set your wit to* match your wit with    101 *impress* impressment,
forced military service    105 *fusty* stale    113–14 *To, Achilles! To,
Ajax! To* Thersites mimicks a driver urging on horses or oxen    119
*brach* bitch    122 *clotpoles* blockheads

I come any more to your tents. I will keep where
there is wit stirring and leave the faction of fools.
*Exit.*

PATROCLUS. A good riddance.                                    125

ACHILLES. Marry, this, sir, is proclaimed through all
  our host:
  That Hector, by the fifth hour of the sun,
  Will, with a trumpet, 'twixt our tents and Troy
  Tomorrow morning call some knight to arms
  That hath a stomach, and such a one that dare      130
  Maintain—I know not what; 'tis trash. Farewell.

AJAX. Farewell? Who shall answer him?

ACHILLES. I know not. 'Tis put to lott'ry. Otherwise,
  He knew his man.

                    [*Exeunt Achilles and Patroclus.*]

AJAX. O, meaning you? I will go learn more of it.   135
                                                 *Exit.*


              ◄§ II. ii §►

[*Troy. Priam's palace.*]*


  *Enter Priam, Hector, Troilus, Paris, and Helenus.*

PRIAM. After so many hours, lives, speeches spent,
  Thus once again says Nestor from the Greeks:
  "Deliver Helen, and all damage else,
  As honor, loss of time, travail, expense,
  Wounds, friends, and what else dear that is con-
    sumed                                              5
  In hot digestion of this cormorant war,
  Shall be struck off." Hector, what say you to't?

HECTOR. Though no man lesser fears the Greeks than
  I,


127 *fifth hour* i.e., 11 A.M.    130 *stomach* appetite for fighting
II.ii.6 *cormorant* ravenous

As far as toucheth my particular,
Yet, dread Priam,                                          10
There is no lady of more softer bowels,
More spongy to suck in the sense of fear,
More ready to cry out, "Who knows what follows?"
Than Hector is. The wound of peace is surety,
Surety secure; but modest doubt is called           15
The beacon of the wise, the tent that searches
To the bottom of the worst. Let Helen go.
Since the first sword was drawn about this question,
Every tithe soul, 'mongst many thousand dismes,
Hath been as dear as Helen. I mean, of ours.        20
If we have lost so many tenths of ours
To guard a thing not ours nor worth to us,
Had it our name, the value of one ten,
What merit's in that reason which denies
The yielding of her up?
TROILUS.                     Fie, fie, my brother!      25
Weigh you the worth and honor of a king
So great as our dread father in a scale
Of common ounces? Will you with counters sum
The past proportion of his infinite,
And buckle in a waist most fathomless              30
With spans and inches so diminutive
As fears and reasons? Fie, for godly shame!
HELENUS. No marvel, though you bite so sharp at rea-
     sons,
You are so empty of them. Should not our father
Bear the great sway of his affairs with reason,    35
Because your speech hath none that tell him so?
TROILUS. You are for dreams and slumbers, brother
     priest;

9 *my particular* me personally   14–15 *The wound . . . secure* the
great danger to peace is too great a sense of security   16 *tent* lint
for probing wounds   19 *Every . . . dismes* every soul taken by war
as its tenth among many thousand such tenths   28 *counters* tokens
used for computation   29 *The past . . . infinite* immeasurability
of his infinite greatness   30 *fathomless* unbounded   31 *spans* a
span was approximately nine inches

You fur your gloves with reason. Here are your
  reasons:
You know an enemy intends you harm;
You know a sword employed is perilous,                    4
And reason flies the object of all harm.
Who marvels then, when Helenus beholds
A Grecian and his sword, if he do set
The very wings of reason to his heels
And fly like chidden Mercury from Jove,                   4
Or like a star disorbed? Nay, if we talk of reason,
Let's shut our gates and sleep! Manhood and honor
Should have hare-hearts, would they but fat their
  thoughts
With this crammed reason. Reason and respect
Make livers pale and lustihood deject.                    5

HECTOR. Brother, she is not worth what she doth cost
  The keeping.
TROILUS.         What's aught but as 'tis valued?
HECTOR. But value dwells not in particular will.
  It holds his estimate and dignity
  As well wherein 'tis precious of itself                 5
  As in the prizer. 'Tis mad idolatry
  To make the service greater than the god;
  (And the will dotes that is attributive
  To what infectiously itself affects,
  Without some image of th' affected merit.)              6
TROILUS. I take today a wife, and my election
  Is led on in the conduct of my will—
  My will enkindled by mine eyes and ears,

---

38 *You fur . . . reason* possibly a proverbial expression; the general
sense is that "you line your gloves with reason thinking it will provide warmth and protection"    41 *object* here, sight    46 *disorbed*
thrown from its sphere    50 *livers* regarded as the seats of passion
53 *particular will* the individual's inclination    54 *his* its    54 *dignity* worth    56 *prizer* one who prizes the thing valued    58–60
*that is attributive . . . merit* that has its source in the will out of its
own contagion loves, without some objective sense of the worth of
the thing loved

Two traded pilots 'twixt the dangerous shores
Of will and judgment. How may I avoid,                    65
Although my will distaste what it elected,
The wife I chose? There can be no evasion
To blench from this and to stand firm by honor.
We turn not back the silks upon the merchant
When we have soiled them, nor the remainder
    viands                                                70
We do not throw in unrespective sieve
Because we now are full. It was thought meet
Paris should do some vengeance on the Greeks.
Your breath with full consent bellied his sails;
The seas and winds, old wranglers, took a truce          75
And did him service; he touched the ports desired,
And for an old aunt whom the Greeks held captive
He brought a Grecian queen, whose youth and
    freshness
Wrinkles Apollo's and makes pale the morning.
Why keep we her? The Grecians keep our aunt.             80
Is she worth keeping? Why, she is a pearl
Whose price hath launched above a thousand ships
And turned crowned kings to merchants.
If you'll avouch 'twas wisdom Paris went—
As you must needs, for you all cried, "Go, go"—           85
If you'll confess he brought home worthy prize—
As you must needs, for you all clapped your hands
And cried, "Inestimable!"—why do you now
The issue of your proper wisdoms rate,
And do a deed that never Fortune did:                     90
Beggar the estimation which you prized
Richer than sea and land? O theft most base,
That we have stol'n what we do fear to keep!
(But thieves unworthy of a thing so stol'n,

---

64 *traded* experienced    68 *blench* flinch    71 *unrespective sieve*
common receptacle    77 *aunt* Hesione, Priam's sister and Ajax's
mother    89 *The issue . . . rate* the offering of your own wisdom
condemn (demean?)    91 *estimation* thing esteemed

That in their country did them that disgrace        95
We fear to warrant in our native place.)

*Enter Cassandra raving with her hair about her ears.*

CASSANDRA. Cry, Troyans, cry!
PRIAM.                    What noise? What shriek
    is this?
TROILUS. 'Tis our mad sister. I do know her voice.
CASSANDRA. Cry, Troyans!
HECTOR. It is Cassandra.        100
CASSANDRA. Cry, Troyans, cry! Lend me ten thousand
    eyes,
And I will fill them with prophetic tears.
HECTOR. Peace, sister, peace!
CASSANDRA. Virgins and boys, mid-age and wrinkled
    eld,
Soft infancy, that nothing canst but cry,        105
Add to my clamors! Let us pay betimes
A moiety of that mass of moan to come.
Cry, Troyans, cry! Practice your eyes with tears!
Troy must not be, nor goodly Ilion stand;
Our firebrand brother, Paris, burns us all.        110
Cry, Troyans, cry! A Helen and a woe!
Cry, cry! Troy burns, or else let Helen go.        *Exit.*
HECTOR. Now, youthful Troilus, do not these high
    strains
Of divination in our sister work
Some touches of remorse? Or is your blood        115
So madly hot that no discourse of reason,
Nor fear of bad success in a bad cause,
Can qualify the same?
TROILUS.                    Why, brother Hector,

95 *disgrace* i.e., the abduction of Helen   96 *warrant* sanction by
continued defense   98 *our mad sister* Cassandra, thought mad because Apollo, after she refused his love, nullified his gift of prophecy
to her by causing others never to believe her   107 *moiety* part
100 *firebrand* when Hecuba was pregnant, with Paris, she dreamed
that she was delivered of a firebrand

We may not think the justness of each act
Such and no other than event doth form it,                        120
Nor once deject the courage of our minds
Because Cassandra's mad. Her brainsick raptures
Cannot distaste the goodness of a quarrel
Which hath our several honors all engaged
To make it gracious. For my private part,                         125
I am no more touched than all Priam's sons;
And Jove forbid there should be done amongst us
Such things as might offend the weakest spleen
To fight for and maintain.
PARIS. Else might the world convince of levity                     130
As well my undertakings as your counsels;
(But I attest the gods, your full consent
Gave wings to my propension and cut off
All fears attending on so dire a project.
For what, alas, can these my single arms?)                        135
What propugnation is in one man's valor
To stand the push and enmity of those
This quarrel would excite? Yet, I protest,
Were I alone to pass the difficulties,
And had as ample power as I have will,                             140
Paris should ne'er retract what he hath done
Nor faint in the pursuit.
PRIAM.                          Paris, you speak
Like one besotted on your sweet delights.
You have the honey still, but these the gall;
So to be valiant is no praise at all.                             145
PARIS. Sir, I propose not merely to myself
The pleasure such a beauty brings with it;
But I would have the soil of her fair rape
Wiped off in honorable keeping her.
What treason were it to the ransacked queen,                      150

122 *brainsick raptures* fits of prophecy    123 *distaste* make distasteful    128 *spleen* temperament    130 *convince* convict    133 *propension* inclination    136 *propugnation* protection    139 *pass* undergo
148 *rape* abduction    150 *ransacked* abducted

Disgrace to your great worths, and shame to me,
Now to deliver her possession up
On terms of base compulsion! Can it be
That so degenerate a strain as this
Should once set footing in your generous bosoms?          15
There's not the meanest spirit on our party
Without a heart to dare or sword to draw
When Helen is defended, nor none so noble
Whose life were ill bestowed or death unfamed
Where Helen is the subject. Then, I say,          16
Well may we fight for her whom we know well
The world's large spaces cannot parallel.*

HECTOR. Paris and Troilus, you have both said well,
And on the cause and question now in hand
Have glozed—but superficially: not much          16
Unlike young men, whom Aristotle thought
Unfit to hear moral philosophy.
The reasons you allege do more conduce
To the hot passion of distempered blood
Than to make up a free determination          17
'Twixt right and wrong; for pleasure and revenge
Have ears more deaf than adders to the voice
Of any true decision. Nature craves
All dues be rendered to their owners. Now,
What nearer debt in all humanity          17
Than wife is to the husband? If this law
Of nature be corrupted through affection,
And that great minds, of partial indulgence
To their benumbèd wills, resist the same,
There is a law in each well-ordered nation          18
To curb those raging appetites that are
Most disobedient and refractory.
If Helen, then, be wife to Sparta's king,

155 *generous* nobly born    165 *glozed* glossed, i.e., commented
167 *moral* i.e., political; Aristotle wrote "political" but throughout
the sixteenth century the word is translated as "moral"    177 *affection* appetite    178 *partial* biased    179 *benumbèd* hypnotized by
appetite

As it is known she is, these moral laws
Of nature and of nations speak aloud                    185
To have her back returned. Thus to persist
In doing wrong extenuates not wrong,
But makes it much more heavy. Hector's opinion
Is this in way of truth.* Yet ne'ertheless,
My spritely brethren, I propend to you                  190
In resolution to keep Helen still;
For 'tis a cause that hath no mean dependence
Upon our joint and several dignities.
TROILUS. Why, there you touched the life of our design!
Were it not glory that we more affected                 195
Than the performance of our heaving spleens,
I would not wish a drop of Troyan blood
Spent more in her defense. But, worthy Hector,
She is a theme of honor and renown,
A spur to valiant and magnanimous deeds,                200
Whose present courage may beat down our foes
And fame in time to come canonize us;
For I presume brave Hector would not lose
So rich advantage of a promised glory
As smiles upon the forehead of this action             205
For the wide world's revenue.
HECTOR.                                I am yours,
You valiant offspring of great Priamus.
I have a roisting challenge sent amongst
The dull and factious nobles of the Greeks
Will strike amazement to their drowsy spirits.          210
I was advertised their great general slept
Whilst emulation in the army crept;
This, I presume, will wake him.            *Exeunt.*

190 *spritely* spirited    190 *propend* incline, here, give in    193 *joint
and several* collective and individual    196 *heaving spleens* unruly
feelings, here, of resentment    208 *roisting* roistering, i.e., boister-
ous    212 *emulation* envious rivalry

### ◄§ II. iii §►

*[The Greek camp. Before Achilles' tent.]*


*Enter Thersites solus.*

THERSITES. How now, Thersites? What, lost in the
labyrinth of thy fury? Shall the elephant Ajax carry
it thus? He beats me, and I rail at him. O worthy
satisfaction! Would it were otherwise—that I could
beat him, whilst he railed at me. 'Sfoot, I'll learn
to conjure and raise devils, but I'll see some issue
of my spiteful execrations. Then there's Achilles, a
rare enginer. If Troy be not taken till these two
undermine it, the walls will stand till they fall of
themselves. O thou great thunder-darter of Olym-
pus, forget that thou art Jove, the king of gods;
and, Mercury, lose all the serpentine craft of thy
caduceus, if ye take not that little, little, less than
little wit from them that they have; which short-
armed ignorance itself knows is so abundant scarce
it will not in circumvention deliver a fly from a
spider, without drawing their massy irons and
cutting the web. After this, the vengeance on the
whole camp! Or, rather, the Neapolitan bone-ache,
for that, methinks, is the curse depending on those
that war for a placket. I have said my prayers,
and devil Envy say "Amen." What ho, my Lord
Achilles!

---

II.iii.2–3 *carry it* carry off the honors   5 *'Sfoot* God's foot   6–7
*but I'll see . . . execrations* rather than not see some result from my
spiteful curses   8 *enginer* soldier used for undermining enemy bat-
tlements   13 *caduceus* Mercury's staff, twined with snakes   19
*Neapolitan bone-ache* syphilis   21 *placket* opening in a petticoat,
hence a loose woman

*Enter Patroclus.*

PATROCLUS. Who's there? Thersites? Good Thersites, come in and rail.                                                    25

THERSITES. If I could 'a' rememb'red a gilt counterfeit, thou wouldst not have slipped out of my contemplation. But it is no matter; thyself upon thyself! The common curse of mankind, folly and ignorance, be thine in great revenue. Heaven bless    30 thee from a tutor, and discipline come not near thee. Let thy blood be thy direction till thy death. Then, if she that lays thee out says thou art a fair corse, I'll be sworn and sworn upon't she never shrouded any but lazars.* Amen. Where's Achilles?    35

PATROCLUS. What, art thou devout? Wast thou in prayer?

THERSITES. Ay, the heavens hear me!

PATROCLUS. Amen.

*Enter Achilles.*

ACHILLES. Who's there?                                          40

PATROCLUS. Thersites, my lord.

ACHILLES. Where? Where? O, where? Art thou come? Why, my cheese, my digestion, why hast thou not served thyself in to my table so many meals? Come, what's Agamemnon?                                             45

THERSITES. Thy commander, Achilles. Then tell me, Patroclus, what's Achilles?

PATROCLUS. Thy lord, Thersites. Then tell me, I pray thee, what's thyself?

THERSITES. Thy knower, Patroclus. Then tell me, Pa-   50 troclus, what art thou?

PATROCLUS. Thou must tell that knowest.

ACHILLES. O tell, tell.

---

27 *slipped* pun on "slip" a counterfeit coin    30 *bless* preserve, guard 32 *blood* violent passion    34 *corse* corpse    35 *lazars* lepers    43 *my cheese, my digestion* calling for cheese as final course of a meal may parallel custom of fool being called in after dinner

THERSITES. I'll decline the whole question. Agamemnon commands Achilles, Achilles is my lord, I am    55
Patroclus' knower, and Patroclus is a fool.

PATROCLUS. You rascal!

THERSITES. Peace, fool! I have not done.

ACHILLES. He is a privileged man. Proceed, Thersites.

THERSITES. Agamemnon is a fool, Achilles is a fool,    60
Thersites is a fool, and, as aforesaid, Patroclus is a
fool.

ACHILLES. Derive this; come.

THERSITES. Agamemnon is a fool to offer to command
Achilles, Achilles is a fool to be commanded of    65
Agamemnon, Thersites is a fool to serve such a
fool, and this Patroclus is a fool positive.

PATROCLUS. Why am I a fool?

THERSITES. Make that demand of the Creator; it suffices
me thou art. Look you, who comes here?    70

*Enter Agamemnon, Ulysses, Nestor, Diomedes,
Ajax, and Calchas.*

ACHILLES. Patroclus, I'll speak with nobody. Come in
with me, Thersites.    *Exit.*

THERSITES. Here is such patchery, such juggling, and
such knavery. All the argument is a whore and a
cuckold, a good quarrel to draw emulous factions    75
and bleed to death upon. Now, the dry serpigo on
the subject, and war and lechery confound all!
                                        [*Exit.*]

AGAMEMNON. Where is Achilles?

PATROCLUS. Within his tent, but ill-disposed, my lord.

AGAMEMNON. Let it be known to him that we are here.    80
He shent our messengers, and we lay by
Our appertainments, visiting of him.
Let him be told so, lest perchance he think

---

54 *decline* run through, i.e., grammatically    59 *privileged* allowed
to speak freely, as said of a professional jester or fool    67 *positive*
absolute    73 *patchery* roguery    76 *serpigo* a skin disease    81
*shent* ill-treated    82 *appertainments* rights of rank

We dare not move the question of our place          85
Or know not what we are.
PATROCLUS.                    I shall so say to him.
                                        [*Exit.*]
ULYSSES. We saw him at the opening of his tent. He is
   not sick.
AJAX. Yes, lion-sick, sick of proud heart. You may
   call it melancholy if you will favor the man; but,
   by my head, 'tis pride. But why, why? Let him show    90
   us a cause. A word, my lord.
                    [*Takes Agamemnon aside.*]
NESTOR. What moves Ajax thus to bay at him?
ULYSSES. Achilles hath inveigled his fool from him.
NESTOR. Who, Thersites?
ULYSSES. He.                                             95
NESTOR. Then will Ajax lack matter, if he have lost his
   argument.
ULYSSES. No, you see, he is his argument that has his
   argument, Achilles.
NESTOR. All the better. Their fraction is more our       100
   wish than their faction. (But it was a strong com-
   posure a fool could disunite.
ULYSSES. The amity that wisdom knits not, folly may
   easily untie.)

   *Enter Patroclus.*

Here comes Patroclus.                                    105
NESTOR. No Achilles with him?
(ULYSSES. The elephant hath joints, but none for cour-
   tesy. His legs are legs for necessity, not for flexure.)
PATROCLUS. Achilles bids me say he is much sorry
   If anything more than your sport and pleasure          110
   Did move your greatness and this noble state
   To call upon him. He hopes it is no other

84 *We dare not . . . place* We (the royal we) dare not assert the
question of our authority    97 *argument* subject matter    100 *fraction* break, i.e., division    101 *faction* union    108 *flexure* bending
111 *state* council of state

But, for your health and your digestion sake,
An after-dinner's breath.

AGAMEMNON.                    Hear you, Patroclus.
We are too well acquainted with these answers;          11
But his evasion, winged thus swift with scorn,
Cannot outfly our apprehensions.
Much attribute he hath, and much the reason
Why we ascribe it to him; yet all his virtues,
(Not virtuously on his own part beheld,)          12
Do in our eyes begin to lose their gloss—
Yea, like fair fruit in an unwholesome dish,
Are like to rot untasted. Go and tell him
We come to speak with him; and you shall not sin
If you do say we think him overproud          12
And underhonest, (in self-assumption greater
Than in the note of judgment, and worthier than
    himself
Here tend the savage strangeness he puts on,
Disguise the holy strength of their command,
And underwrite in an observing kind          13
His humorous predominance; yea, watch
His pettish lunes, his ebbs and flows, as if
The passage and whole carriage of this action
Rode on his tide.) Go tell him this; and add
That, if he overhold his price so much,          13
We'll none of him; (but let him, like an engine
Not portable, lie under this report:
"Bring action hither, this cannot go to war.")
A stirring dwarf we do allowance give
Before a sleeping giant. Tell him so.          140

114 *breath* gentle exercise    120 *Not . . . beheld* not modestly borne
126 *underhonest* not sufficiently candid    127 *the note of judgment*
the mark of good judgment    128 *tend the savage strangeness* wait
upon the rude aloofness    129–31 *Disguise . . . predominance* disguise the divine power of their authority and subscribe by passive
attendance to his capricious assertion of superiority    132 *pettish
lunes* petulant fits of temper    135 *overhold* overvalue    136 *engine*
here, military    139 *allowance* approbation

PATROCLUS. I shall, and bring his answer presently.
                                                   [*Exit.*]
AGAMEMNON. In second voice we'll not be satisfied;
    (We come to speak with him.) Ulysses, enter you.
                                          *Exit Ulysses.*
AJAX. What is he more than another?
AGAMEMNON. No more than what he thinks he is.         145
AJAX. Is he so much? Do you not think he thinks
    himself a better man than I am?
AGAMEMNON. No question.
AJAX. Will you subscribe his thought, and say he is?
AGAMEMNON. No, noble Ajax; you are as strong, as      150
    valiant, as wise, no less noble, much more gentle,
    and altogether more tractable.
AJAX. Why should a man be proud? How doth pride
    grow? I know not what pride is.
AGAMEMNON. Your mind is the clearer and your vir-     155
    tues the fairer. He that is proud eats up himself.
    Pride is his own glass, his own trumpet, his own
    chronicle; and whatever praises itself but in the
    deed, devours the deed in the praise.

    *Enter Ulysses.*

AJAX. I do hate a proud man as I hate the engend'r-   160
    ing of toads.
NESTOR. [*Aside*] And yet he loves himself. Is't not
    strange?
ULYSSES. Achilles will not to the field tomorrow.
AGAMEMNON. What's his excuse?
ULYSSES.                        He doth rely on none,  165
    (But carries on the stream of his dispose
    Without observance or respect of any,
    In will peculiar and in self-admission.)
AGAMEMNON. Why will he not upon our fair request
    Untent his person and share th'air with us?        170

---

157 *glass* mirror    166 *dispose* bent of mind    168 *peculiar* determined by himself alone    168 *self-admission* by his own approval

ULYSSES. (Things small as nothing, for request's sake
    only,
    He makes important. Possessed he is with great-
        ness,
    And speaks not to himself but with a pride
    That quarrels at self-breath. Imagined worth
    Holds in his blood such swoln and hot discourse          175
    That 'twixt his mental and his active parts
    Kingdomed Achilles in commotion rages
    And batters down himself.) What should I say?
    He is so plaguy proud that the death-tokens of it
    Cry "No recovery."
AGAMEMNON.          Let Ajax go to him.                       180
    Dear lord, go you and greet him in his tent;
    'Tis said he holds you well, and will be led
    At your request a little from himself.
ULYSSES. O Agamemnon, let it not be so!
    We'll consecrate the steps that Ajax makes                185
    When they go from Achilles. Shall the proud lord
    That bastes his arrogance with his own seam
    (And never suffers matter of the world
    Enter his thoughts, save such as doth revolve
    And ruminate himself)—shall he be worshiped             190
    Of that we hold an idol more than he?
    No, this thrice-worthy and right valiant lord
    Shall not so stale his palm, (nobly acquired,
    Nor, by my will, assubjugate his merit,
    As amply titled as Achilles' is,)                        195
    By going to Achilles.
    That were to enlard his fat-already pride,
    (And add more coals to Cancer when he burns
    With entertaining great Hyperion.)

171 *for request's sake only* only because they are requested    174
*self-breath* merely because he spoke    177 *Kingdomed* i.e., compar-
ing Achilles to a kingdom at war with itself    179 *death-tokens*
marks of the plague on the body    187 *seam* fat    193 *stale his
palm* sully his glory    194 *assubjugate* debase    198 *Cancer* i.e.,
summer    199 *Hyperion* the sun

This lord go to him! Jupiter forbid,                              200
And say in thunder, "Achilles, go to him."

NESTOR. [*Aside*] O, this is well. He rubs the vein of
him.

DIOMEDES. [*Aside*] And how his silence drinks up his
applause!

AJAX. If I go to him, with my armèd fist
I'll pash him o'er the face.                                      205

AGAMEMNON. O, no! You shall not go.

AJAX. An he be proud with me, I'll pheese his pride.
Let me go to him.

ULYSSES. Not for the worth that hangs upon our quarrel.

AJAX. A paltry, insolent fellow!                                  210

NESTOR. [*Aside*] How he describes himself!

AJAX. Can he not be sociable?

ULYSSES. [*Aside*] The raven chides blackness.

AJAX. I'll let his humor's blood.

AGAMEMNON. [*Aside*] He will be the physician that       215
should be the patient.

AJAX. An all men were of my mind——

ULYSSES. [*Aside*] Wit would be out of fashion.

AJAX. 'A should not bear it so, 'a should eat swords
first! Shall pride carry it?                                      220

NESTOR. [*Aside*] An 'twould, you'd carry half.

ULYSSES. [*Aside*] 'A would have ten shares.

AJAX. I will knead him; I'll make him supple.

NESTOR. [*Aside*] He's not yet through warm. Force
him with praises; pour in, pour, his ambition is dry.   225

ULYSSES. [*To Agamemnon*] My lord, you feed too
much on this dislike.

NESTOR. Our noble general, do not do so.

DIOMEDES. You must prepare to fight without Achilles.

ULYSSES. Why, 'tis this naming of him does him harm.

---

202 *vein* mood    205 *pash* smash    207 *pheese* take care of, settle
214 *let his humor's blood* cure his humor of pride by letting blood
224 *through* thoroughly    224 *Force* stuff

Here is a man—but 'tis before his face;    230
I will be silent.

NESTOR.    Wherefore should you so?
He is not emulous, as Achilles is.

ULYSSES. Know the whole world, he is as valiant——

AJAX. A whoreson dog, that shall palter with us thus!
Would he were a Troyan!    235

NESTOR. What a vice were it in Ajax now——

ULYSSES. If he were proud——

DIOMEDES. Or covetous of praise——

ULYSSES. Ay, or surly borne——

DIOMEDES. Or strange, or self-affected!    240

ULYSSES. Thank the heavens, lord, thou art of sweet
    composure;
Praise him that got thee, she that gave thee suck;
Famed be thy tutor, and thy parts of nature
Thrice-famed beyond, beyond all erudition;
But he that disciplined thine arms to fight,    245
Let Mars divide eternity in twain
And give him half; and, for thy vigor,
Bull-bearing Milo his addition yield
To sinewy Ajax. I will not praise thy wisdom,
Which, like a bourn, a pale, a shore, confines    250
Thy spacious and dilated parts. Here's Nestor,
Instructed by the antiquary times,
He must, he is, he cannot but be wise;
But pardon, father Nestor, were your days
As green as Ajax, and your brain so tempered,    255
You should not have the eminence of him,
But be as Ajax.

AJAX.    Shall I call you father?

NESTOR. Ay, my good son.

---

232 *emulous* envious    234 *palter* deal crookedly    240 *strange, or*
*self-affected* aloof or self-centered    243 *parts of nature* natural
attributes    248 *Milo* a Greek athlete famous for bearing a bull on
his shoulders, hence his addition or epithet, 'Bull-bearing'    250
*a bourn, a pale* a boundary, a fence    256 *have the eminence* be
superior to

DIOMEDES.                    Be ruled by him, Lord Ajax.
ULYSSES. There is no tarrying here; the hart Achilles
  Keeps thicket. Please it our great general                260
  To call together all his state of war;
  Fresh kings are come to Troy. Tomorrow,
  We must with all our main of power stand fast.
  And here's a lord—come knights from east to west,
  And cull their flower, Ajax shall cope the best.         265
AGAMEMNON. Go we to council. Let Achilles sleep;
  Light boats sail swift, though greater hulks draw
      deep.                                      *Exeunt.*


### ᵉᶳ III. i ᶫᵉ

[*Troy. Paris' antechamber in Priam's palace.*]


*Music sounds within. Enter Pandarus and a Servant.*

PANDARUS. Friend you, pray you a word. Do you not
  follow the young Lord Paris?
SERVANT. Ay, sir, when he goes before me.
PANDARUS. You depend upon him, I mean.
SERVANT. Sir, I do depend upon the Lord.                    5
PANDARUS. You depend upon a notable gentleman; I
  must needs praise him.
SERVANT. The Lord be praised!
PANDARUS. You know me, do you not?
SERVANT. Faith, sir, superficially.                         10
PANDARUS. Friend, know me better. I am the Lord
  Pandarus.
SERVANT. I hope I shall know your honor better.
PANDARUS. I do desire it.
SERVANT. You are in the state of grace.                     15

261 *state* noblemen in council    263 *main* full might    265 *cope*
meet    III.i.4 *depend upon* be servant of    15 *state of grace* bounti-
ful liberality of God; Servant quibbles on "grace" insinuating (1)
God's grace (2) wish for gratuity (3) respect for ducal title

PANDARUS. Grace? Not so, friend. Honor and lord-
ship are my titles. What music is this?

SERVANT. I do but partly know, sir. It is music in
parts.

PANDARUS. Know you the musicians?                    20

SERVANT. Wholly, sir.

PANDARUS. Who play they to?

SERVANT. To the hearers, sir.

PANDARUS. At whose pleasure, friend?

SERVANT. At mine, sir, and theirs that love music.   25

PANDARUS. Command, I mean, friend.

SERVANT. Who shall I command, sir?

PANDARUS. Friend, we understand not one another. I
am too courtly, and thou too cunning. At whose
request do these men play?                           30

SERVANT. That's to't, indeed, sir. Marry, sir, at the request of Paris, my lord, who is there in person;
with him the mortal Venus, the heartblood of
beauty, love's invisible soul.

PANDARUS. Who? My cousin Cressida?                    35

SERVANT. No, sir, Helen. Could not you find out that
by her attributes?

PANDARUS. It should seem, fellow, that thou hast not
seen the Lady Cressid. I come to speak with
Paris from the Prince Troilus. I will make a com-   40
plimental assault upon him, for my business
seethes.

SERVANT. Sodden business! There's a stewed phrase,
indeed.

   *Enter Paris and Helen.*

PANDARUS. Fair be to you, my lord, and to all this fair   45
company. Fair desires in all fair measure fairly
guide them. Especially to you, fair queen, fair
thoughts be your fair pillow.

18–19 *in parts* in harmony    42 *seethes* boils, i.e., demands haste
43 *Sodden . . . stewed* boiled, hence pertaining to stews, i.e., brothels
47 *queen* possible quibble on quean, i.e., slut

HELEN. Dear lord, you are full of fair words.

PANDARUS. You speak your fair pleasure, sweet queen.    50
Fair prince, here is good broken music.

PARIS. You have broke it, cousin; and, by my life, you
shall make it whole again; you shall piece it out
with a piece of your performance. Nell, he is full
of harmony.    55

PANDARUS. Truly, lady, no.

HELEN. O, sir!

PANDARUS. Rude, in sooth; in good sooth, very rude.

PARIS. Well said, my lord. (Well, you say so in fits.)

PANDARUS. I have business to my lord, dear queen. My    60
lord, will you vouchsafe me a word?

HELEN. Nay, this shall not hedge us out. We'll hear you
sing, certainly.

PANDARUS. Well, sweet queen, you are pleasant with
me. But, marry, thus, my lord: my dear lord and    65
most esteemed friend, your brother Troilus——

HELEN. My Lord Pandarus, honey-sweet lord——

PANDARUS. Go to, sweet queen, go to—commends himself most affectionately to you.

HELEN. You shall not bob us out of our melody. If    70
you do, our melancholy upon your head!

PANDARUS. Sweet queen, sweet queen, that's a sweet
queen, i' faith.

HELEN. And to make a sweet lady sad is a sour offense.

PANDARUS. Nay, that shall not serve your turn; that    75
shall it not, in truth, la. Nay, I care not for such
words; no, no. And, my lord, he desires you that,
if the king call for him at supper, you will make his
excuse.

HELEN. My Lord Pandarus——    80

PANDARUS. What says my sweet queen, my very, very
sweet queen?

PARIS. What exploit's in hand? Where sups he tonight?

HELEN. Nay, but my Lord——

51 *broken music* (1)music in parts (2)music by combination of
different instruments(?)    59 *fits* sections of a song    70 *bob* cheat

PANDARUS. What says my sweet queen? My cousin will    85
fall out with you.

HELEN. You must not know where he sups.

PARIS. I'll lay my life, with my disposer Cressida.

PANDARUS. No, no; no such matter; you are wide.
Come, your disposer is sick.    90

PARIS. Well, I'll make excuse.

PANDARUS. Ay, good my lord. Why should you say
Cressida? No, your poor disposer's sick.

PARIS. I spy.

PANDARUS. You spy? What do you spy? Come, give    95
me an instrument now, sweet queen.

HELEN. Why, this is kindly done.

PANDARUS. My niece is horribly in love with a thing
you have, sweet queen.

HELEN. She shall have it, my lord, if it be not my Lord    100
Paris.

PANDARUS. He? No, she'll none of him; they two are
twain.

HELEN. Falling in, after falling out, may make them
three.    105

PANDARUS. Come, come, I'll hear no more of this. I'll
sing you a song now.

HELEN. Ay, ay, prithee. Now by my troth, sweet lord,
thou hast a fine forehead.

PANDARUS. Ay, you may, you may.    110

HELEN. Let thy song be love. This love will undo us all.
O Cupid, Cupid, Cupid!

PANDARUS. Love! Ay, that it shall, i' faith.

PARIS. Ay, good now, "Love, love, nothing but love."

PANDARUS. In good troth, it begins so:    [Sings.]    115
Love, love, nothing but love, still love still more!
For, O, love's bow shoots buck and doe.
The shaft confounds not that it wounds,

---

85 *My cousin* i.e., Paris    88 *disposer* i.e., one who controls; meaning here is uncertain    89 *wide* wide of the mark    103 *twain* at
odds    110 *you may* i.e., have your joke    118 *that* because

But tickles still the sore.
These lovers cry, O ho! they die!                              120
Yet that which seems the wound to kill
Doth turn O ho! to Ha, ha, he!
So dying love lives still.
O ho! a while, but Ha, ha, ha!
O ho! groans out for Ha, ha, ha!—Heigh ho!                     125

HELEN. In love, i' faith, to the very tip of the nose.

PARIS. He eats nothing but doves, love, and that breeds
hot blood, and hot blood begets hot thoughts, and
hot thoughts beget hot deeds, and hot deeds is love.

PANDARUS. Is this the generation of love—hot blood,            130
hot thoughts, and hot deeds? Why, they are vipers.
Is love a generation of vipers? Sweet lord, who's
a-field today?

PARIS. Hector, Deiphobus, Helenus, Antenor, and all
the gallantry of Troy. I would fain have armed            135
today, but my Nell would not have it so. How
chance my brother Troilus went not?

HELEN. He hangs the lip at something.* You know all,
Lord Pandarus.

PANDARUS. Not I, honey-sweet queen. I long to hear            140
how they sped today. You'll remember your
brother's excuse?

PARIS. To a hair.

PANDARUS. Farewell, sweet queen.

HELEN. Commend me to your niece.                               145

PANDARUS. I will, sweet queen.   [*Exit.*] *Sound a retreat.*

PARIS. They're come from the field. Let us to Priam's
hall
To greet the warriors. Sweet Helen, I must woo you
To help unarm our Hector. His stubborn buckles,
With these your white enchanting fingers touched,         150
Shall more obey than to the edge of steel
Or force of Greekish sinews. You shall do more
Than all the island kings—disarm great Hector.

119 *sore* wound, also buck in his fourth year    153 *island* Greek

HELEN. 'Twill make us proud to be his servant, Paris;
  Yea, what he shall receive of us in duty                              155
  Gives us more palm in beauty than we have,
  Yea, overshines ourself.
PARIS. Sweet above thought I love thee.          *Exeunt.*


### ⋙ III. ii ⋘

[*Troy. Pandarus' orchard.*]


    *Enter Pandarus and Troilus' Man.*

PANDARUS. How now, where's thy master? At my
  cousin Cressida's?
MAN. No, sir; he stays for you to conduct him thither.

    *Enter Troilus.*

PANDARUS. O, here he comes. How now, how now?
TROILUS. Sirrah, walk off.                    [*Exit Man.*]     5
PANDARUS. Have you seen my cousin?
TROILUS. No, Pandarus. I stalk about her door
  Like a strange soul upon the Stygian banks
  Staying for waftage. O, be thou my Charon,
  And give me swift transportance to those fields     10
  Where I may wallow in the lily beds
  Proposed for the deserver. O gentle Pandar,
  From Cupid's shoulder pluck his painted wings,
  And fly with me to Cressid.
PANDARUS. Walk here i' th' orchard. I'll bring her     15
  straight.                            *Exit Pandarus.*
TROILUS. I am giddy; expectation whirls me round.
  ✓Th' imaginary relish is so sweet
  That it enchants my sense. What will it be

III.ii.8 *Stygian* of Styx, the river across which Charon ferried the
dead   9 *waftage* passage   10 *those fields* Elysian fields   12 *Proposed* promised

When that the wat'ry palates taste indeed
Love's thrice-repurèd nectar? Death, I fear me,
Sounding* destruction, or some joy too fine,
Too subtle, potent, tuned too sharp in sweetness
For the capacity of my ruder powers.
I fear it much; and I do fear besides          25
That I shall lose distinction in my joys,
As doth a battle, when they charge on heaps
The enemy flying.

    *Enter Pandarus.*

PANDARUS. She's making her ready; she'll come
straight; you must be witty now. She does so blush,     30
and fetches her wind so short as if she were frayed
with a spirit. I'll fetch her. It is the prettiest villain; she fetches her breath as short as a new-
ta'en sparrow.                          *Exit Pandarus.*

TROILUS. Even such a passion doth embrace my bosom.   35
My heart beats thicker than a feverous pulse,
And all my powers do their bestowing lose,
Like vassalage at unawares encount'ring
The eye of majesty.

    *Enter Pandarus and Cressida.*

PANDARUS. Come, come, what need you blush? Shame's    40
a baby. Here she is now; swear the oaths now to
her that you have sworn to me. What! Are you
gone again? You must be watched ere you be made
tame, must you? Come your ways, come your
ways; an you draw backward, we'll put you i' the    45
fills. Why do you not speak to her? Come, draw
this curtain, and let's see your picture. Alas the
day, how loath you are to offend daylight! An

---

22 *Sounding* swooning    30 *be witty* have your wits about you
31–32 *frayed with a spirit* frightened by a ghost    37 *bestowing*
proper use    43 *watched* kept awake, as in the taming of hawks
46 *fills* shafts of a cart    47 *curtain . . . picture* in Shakespeare's
day paintings were usually covered; here curtain=veil, picture=face

'twere dark, you'd close sooner. So, so; rub on, 50
and kiss the mistress. How now, a kiss in fee-
farm! Build there, carpenter; the air is sweet.
Nay, you shall fight your hearts out ere I part you.
The falcon as the tercel, for all the ducks i' the
river. Go to, go to.

TROILUS. You have bereft me of all words, lady. 55

PANDARUS. Words pay no debts, give her deeds; but
she'll bereave you o' the deeds too if she call your
activity in question. What, billing again? Here's "In
witness whereof the parties interchangeably"—
Come in, come in. I'll go get a fire.    [*Exit*.] 60

CRESSIDA. Will you walk in, my lord?

TROILUS. O Cressid, how often have I wished me thus!

CRESSIDA. Wished, my lord? The gods grant—O my
lord!

TROILUS. What should they grant? What makes this 65
pretty abruption? What too curious dreg espies
my sweet lady in the fountain of our love?

CRESSIDA. More dregs than water, if my fears have
eyes.

TROILUS. Fears make devils of cherubins; they never 70
see truly.

CRESSIDA. Blind fear, that seeing reason leads, finds
safer footing than blind reason stumbling without
fear. To fear the worst oft cures the worse.

TROILUS. O, let my lady apprehend no fear; in all 75
Cupid's pageant there is presented no monster.

CRESSIDA. Nor nothing monstrous neither?

TROILUS. Nothing but our undertakings when we vow
to weep seas, live in fire, eat rocks, tame tigers,

49–50 *rub . . . mistress* in bowling "to rub" was to meet obstacles
in the way of the small object-ball called the "mistress"    50–51 *in
fee-farm* in perpetuity    53–54 *The falcon . . . tercel* I will bet
on the falcon, i.e., the female, against the tercel, i.e., the male
58–59 *"In witness . . . interchangeably"* a legal formula, usually
ending with the words "have set their hands and seals"    66 *abruption* breaking off    66 *too curious* overly cautious or especially
minute

thinking it harder for our mistress to devise imposi-    80
tion enough than for us to undergo any difficulty
imposed. This is the monstruosity in love, lady,
that the will is infinite and the execution confined;
that the desire is boundless and the act a slave to
limit.                                                    85

CRESSIDA. They say all lovers swear more performance than they are able, and yet reserve an ability
that they never perform, vowing more than the
perfection of ten and discharging less than the
tenth part of one. They that have the voice of     90
lions and the act of hares—are they not monsters?

TROILUS. Are there such? Such are not we. Praise us
as we are tasted, allow us as we prove; our head
shall go bare till merit crown it. (No perfection in
reversion shall have a praise in present;) we will     95
not name desert before his birth, and, being born,
his addition shall be humble. Few words to fair
faith. Troilus shall be such to Cressid, as what envy
can say worst shall be a mock for his truth, and
what truth can speak truest not truer than Troilus.   100

CRESSIDA. Will you walk in, my lord?

*Enter Pandarus.\**

PANDARUS. What, blushing still? Have you not done
talking yet?

CRESSIDA. Well, uncle, what folly I commit, I dedicate
to you.                                                   105

PANDARUS. I thank you for that. If my lord get a boy
of you, you'll give him me. Be true to my lord;
if he flinch, chide me for it.

TROILUS. You know now your hostages: your uncle's
word and my firm faith.                                   110

PANDARUS. Nay, I'll give my word for her too. Our
kindred, though they be long ere they be wooed,

93 *tasted* tested    95 *reversion* right of future possession    98–100
*as what envy . . . truth* so that the worst envy can say will serve
only as a mockery of his, i.e., Troilus's constancy

they are constant being won. They are burrs, I can
tell you; they'll stick where they are thrown.

CRESSIDA. Boldness comes to me now and brings me
heart.                                                    11

Prince Troilus, I have loved you night and day
For many weary months.

TROILUS. Why was my Cressid then so hard to win?

CRESSIDA. Hard to seem won; but I was won, my lord,
With the first glance that ever—pardon me;              12
If I confess much you will play the tyrant.
I love you now, but, till now, not so much
But I might master it. In faith, I lie;
My thoughts were like unbridled children grown
Too headstrong for their mother. See, we fools!        12
Why have I blabbed? Who shall be true to us
When we are so unsecret to ourselves?
But, though I loved you well, I wooed you not;
And yet, good faith, I wished myself a man,
Or that we women had men's privilege                   13
Of speaking first. Sweet, bid me hold my tongue,
For in this rapture I shall surely speak
The thing I shall repent. See, see! Your silence,
Cunning in dumbness, from my weakness draws
My very soul of counsel. Stop my mouth.                13

TROILUS. And shall, albeit sweet music issues thence.

PANDARUS. Pretty, i'faith.

CRESSIDA. My lord, I do beseech you, pardon me;
'Twas not my purpose thus to beg a kiss.
I am ashamed. O heavens, what have I done?             14
For this time will I take my leave, my lord.

TROILUS. Your leave, sweet Cressid?

PANDARUS. Leave! An you take leave till tomorrow
morning——

CRESSIDA. Pray you, content you.

TROILUS.                        What offends you, lady?  14

CRESSIDA. Sir, mine own company.

TROILUS. You cannot shun yourself.

135 *soul of counsel* inmost thought

CRESSIDA. Let me go and try.
  I have a kind of self resides with you;
  But an unkind self, that itself will leave       150
  To be another's fool. I would be gone.
  Where is my wit? I know not what I speak.
TROILUS. Well know they what they speak that speak
  so wisely.
CRESSIDA. Perchance, my lord, I show more craft than
  love,
  And fell so roundly to a large confession       155
  To angle for your thoughts. But you are wise,
  Or else you love not, for to be wise and love
  Exceeds man's might; that dwells with gods above.
TROILUS. O that I thought it could be in a woman—
  As, if it can, I will presume in you—       160
  To feed for aye her lamp and flames of love;
  To keep her constancy in plight and youth,
  (Outliving beauty's outward, with a mind
  That doth renew swifter than blood decays;)
  Or that persuasion could but thus convince me       165
  That my integrity and truth to you
  Might be affronted with the match and weight
  Of such a winnowed purity in love:
  How were I then uplifted! But, alas,
  I am as true as truth's simplicity,       170
  And simpler than the infancy of truth.
CRESSIDA. In that I'll war with you.
TROILUS.                O virtuous fight,
  When right with right wars who shall be most right!
  True swains in love shall in the world to come
  Approve their truth by Troilus. When their
  rhymes,       175

155 *roundly* frankly   155 *large* unrestrained   156–58 *But you are wise . . . man's might* no generally accepted interpretation of this passage exists; the text may be corrupt, for Cressida appears to contradict herself   162 *in plight and youth* in its first promise and freshness   164 *blood* passion   167 *affronted* met   175 *Approve* attest

Full of protest, of oath and big compare,
Wants similes, truth tired with iteration,
"As true as steel, as plantage to the moon,
As sun to day, as turtle to her mate,
As iron to adamant, as earth to the center," 180
Yet, after all comparisons of truth,
(As truth's authentic author to be cited,)
"As true as Troilus" shall crown up the verse
And sanctify the numbers.

CRESSIDA.                    Prophet may you be!
If I be false or swerve a hair from truth, 185
When time is old and hath forgot itself,
When waterdrops have worn the stones of Troy,
And blind oblivion swallowed cities up,
And mighty states characterless are grated
To dusty nothing, yet let memory, 190
From false to false among false maids in love,
Upbraid my falsehood! When they've said, "As false
As air, as water, wind or sandy earth,
As fox to lamb, as wolf to heifer's calf,
Pard to the hind, or stepdame to her son," 195
Yea, let them say, to stick the heart of falsehood,
"As false as Cressid."

PANDARUS. Go to, a bargain made. Seal it, seal it; I'll
be the witness. Here I hold your hand, here my
cousin's. If ever you prove false one to another, 200
since I have taken such pains to bring you together, let all pitiful goers-between be called to the
world's end after my name; call them all Pandars.
Let all constant men be Troiluses, all false women
Cressids, and all brokers-between Pandars! Say, 205
"Amen."

TROILUS. Amen.

CRESSIDA. Amen.

177 Wants lacks    178 plantage plants or vegetation whose growth,
according to popular belief, was influenced by the moon    179 turtle
turtledove    180 adamant magnetic loadstone    184 numbers verses
189 characterless unmarked    195 Pard leopard    195 hind doe

PANDARUS. Amen. Whereupon I will show you a chamber which bed, because it shall not speak of your   210
pretty encounters, press it to death. Away!
                    *Exeunt* [*Troilus and Cressida*].
And Cupid grant all tongue-tied maidens here
Bed, chamber, Pandar to provide this gear!   *Exit.**


        ⋙ III. iii ⋘

[*The Greek camp. Before Achilles' tent.*]


    Enter Ulysses, Diomedes, Nestor, Agamemnon,
    [*Menelaus, Ajax, and*] *Calchas. Flourish* [*of
    trumpets.*]

CALCHAS. Now, princes, for the service I have done,
    Th' advantage of the time prompts me aloud
    To call for recompense. Appear it to mind
    That (through the sight I bear in things to come,)
    I have abandoned Troy, left my possession,          5
    Incurred a traitor's name, exposed myself,
    From certain and possessed conveniences,
    To doubtful fortunes, sequest'ring from me all
    That time, acquaintance, custom, and condition
    Made tame and most familiar to my nature;          10
    And here, to do you service, am become
    As new into the world, strange, unacquainted.
    I do beseech you, as in way of taste,
    To give me now a little benefit
    Out of those many registered in promise,           15
    Which, you say, live to come in my behalf.
AGAMEMNON. What wouldst thou of us, Troyan? Make
    demand.


210 *because* so that   III.iii.4 *sight* foresight   8 *sequest'ring* putting aside   10 *tame* familiar   13 *taste* foretaste

CALCHAS. You have a Troyan prisoner, called Antenor,
    Yesterday took; Troy holds him very dear.
    Oft have you—often have you thanks therefor—    20
    Desired my Cressid in right great exchange,
    Whom Troy hath still denied; but this Antenor
    (I know) is such a (wrest in their affairs
    That their negotiations all must slack,
    Wanting his manage; and)* they will almost    2.
    Give us a prince of blood, a son of Priam,
    In change of him. Let him be sent, great princes,
    And he shall buy my daughter; and her presence
    Shall quite strike off all service I have done
    In most accepted pain.
AGAMEMNON.                Let Diomedes bear him,    3
    And bring us Cressid hither; Calchas shall have
    What he requests of us. Good Diomed,
    Furnish you fairly, for this interchange.
    Withal bring word if Hector will tomorrow
    Be answered in his challenge. Ajax is ready.    3!
DIOMEDES. This shall I undertake, and 'tis a burden
    Which I am proud to bear.        Exit [with Calchas].

    Enter Achilles and Patroclus [and] stand in their
    tent.

ULYSSES. Achilles stands i' th' entrance of his tent.
    Please it our general pass strangely by him,
    As if he were forgot; and, princes all,    4
    Lay negligent and loose regard upon him.
    I will come last. 'Tis like he'll question me
    Why such unplausive eyes are bent, why turned,
    on him.
    If so, I have derision medicinable
    To use between your strangeness and his pride,    4!
    (Which his own will shall have desire to drink.

---

22 *still* always    23 *wrest* key for tuning a harp and possibly other
stringed instruments, hence a key to harmony    30 *accepted* cheer-
fully endured    39 *strangely* aloofly    43 *unplausive* disapproving

It may do good; pride hath no other glass
To show itself but pride, for supple knees
Feed arrogance and are the proud man's fees.)
AGAMEMNON. We'll execute your purpose, and put on    50
  A form of strangeness as we pass along.
  So do each lord, and either greet him not
  Or else disdainfully, which shall shake him more
  Than if not looked on. I will lead the way.*
ACHILLES. What comes the general to speak with me?    55
  You know my mind; I'll fight no more 'gainst Troy.
AGAMEMNON. What says Achilles? Would he aught
  with us?
NESTOR. Would you, my lord, aught with the general?
ACHILLES. No.
NESTOR. Nothing, my lord.                              60
AGAMEMNON. The better.
ACHILLES. Good day, good day.
MENELAUS. How do you? How do you?
ACHILLES. What, does the cuckold scorn me?
AJAX. How now, Patroclus?                              65
ACHILLES. Good morrow, Ajax.
AJAX. Ha?
ACHILLES. Good morrow.
AJAX. Ay, and good next day too.          *Exeunt.*
ACHILLES. What mean these fellows? Know they not
  Achilles?                                         70
PATROCLUS. They pass by strangely. They were used to
  bend,
  To send their smiles before them to Achilles,
  To come as humbly as they used to creep
  To holy altars.
ACHILLES.          What, am I poor of late?
  'Tis certain, greatness, once fall'n out with fortune,  75
  Must fall out with men too. (What the declined is
  He shall as soon read in the eyes of others

47–48 *pride . . . pride* pride has no other mirror in which to see
itself but very pride itself

As feel in his own fall; for men, like butterflies,
Show not their mealy wings but to the summer,
And not a man, for being simply man,                         80
Hath any honor, but honor for those honors
That are without him, as place, riches, and favor,
Prizes of accident as oft as merit;
Which when they fall, as being slippery standers,
The love that leaned on them as slippery too,               85
Doth one pluck down another, and together
Die in the fall.) But 'tis not so with me;
Fortune and I are friends. I do enjoy
At ample point all that I did possess,
Save these men's looks—who do, methinks, find out    90
Something not worth in me such rich beholding
As they have often given. Here is Ulysses;
I'll interrupt his reading.
How now, Ulysses.

ULYSSES.                    Now, great Thetis' son.

ACHILLES. What are you reading?

ULYSSES.                              A strange fellow here      95
Writes me that man, how dearly ever parted,
(How much in having, or without or in,)
Cannot make boast to have that which he hath,
Nor feels not what he owes but by reflection;
(As when his virtues aiming upon others                   100
Heat them, and they retort that heat again
To the first giver.)

ACHILLES.                This is not strange, Ulysses.
The beauty that is borne here in the face
The bearer knows not, (but commends itself
To others' eyes; nor doth the eye itself,                  105
That most pure spirit of sense, behold itself,
Not going from itself; but eye to eye opposed
Salutes each other with each other's form;

79 *mealy* powdery    82 *without* external to    89 *At ample point*
fully    96 *how dearly ever parted* howsoever abundantly talented
97 *How much . . . or in* however much he possesses, either outside
of himself or within himself    99 *owes* owns

For speculation turns not to itself)
Till it hath traveled (and is married there)*          110
Where it may see itself. This is not strange at all.

ULYSSES. I do not strain at the position—
It is familiar—but at the author's drift;
Who in his circumstance expressly proves
That no man is the lord of anything—                   115
(Though in and of him there be much consisting—)
Till he communicate his parts to others.
(Nor doth he of himself know them for aught
Till he behold them formed in th' applause
Where they're extended; who, like an arch, rever-
     b'rate                                            120
The voice again, or, like a gate of steel
Fronting the sun, receives and renders back
His figure and his heat.) I was much rapt in this,
And apprehended here immediately
Th' unknown Ajax.                                       125
Heavens, what a man is there! A very horse,
That has he knows not what. (Nature, what things
     there are
Most abject in regard and dear in use!
What things again most dear in the esteem
And poor in worth!) Now shall we see tomorrow,         130
An act that very chance doth throw upon him:
Ajax renowned. O heavens, what some men do,
While some men leave to do!
How some men creep in skittish Fortune's hall,
Whiles others play the idiots in her eyes!             135
(How one man eats into another's pride,
While pride is fasting in his wantonness!)

109 *speculation* power of sight    112 *position* i.e., of the writer
114 *circumstance* detailed discussion    116 *Though . . . consisting*
though much exists in him and because of him    119-20 *Till . . .
extended* Till he sees them, i.e., his qualities shaped in the form of
the applause wherever they (the qualities) are projected    120 W*ho*
which, i.e., the applause    128 *Most . . . use* despised in esteem
and yet valuable in use    134 *in* into    134 *skittish* i.e., unreliable
137 *his wantonness* its own wanton self-satisfaction

To see these Grecian lords—why, even already
They clap the lubber Ajax on the shoulder,
As if his foot were on brave Hector's breast,                    14
And great Troy shrinking.
ACHILLES. I do believe it; for they passed by me
As misers do by beggars, neither gave to me
Good word nor look. What, are my deeds forgot?
ULYSSES. Time hath, my lord, a wallet at his back,              14
Wherein he puts alms for oblivion,
A great-sized monster of ingratitudes.
Those scraps are good deeds past, which are de-
    voured
As fast as they are made, forgot as soon
As done. Perseverance, dear my lord,                           15
Keeps honor bright. To have done, is to hang
Quite out of fashion, like a rusty mail
In monumental mock'ry. Take the instant way;
For honor travels in a strait so narrow
Where one but goes abreast. Keep, then, the path;             15
For emulation hath a thousand sons
That one by one pursue. If you give way,
Or hedge aside from the direct forthright,
Like to an ent'red tide they all rush by
And leave you hindmost;                                         16
Or, like a gallant horse fall'n in first rank,
Lie there for pavement to the abject rear,
O'errun and trampled on. Then what they do in
    present,
Though less than yours in past, must o'ertop yours.
For time is like a fashionable host,                            16
That slightly shakes his parting guest by the hand,
And with his arms outstretched, as he would fly,
Grasps in the comer. The welcome ever smiles,
And farewell goes out sighing. Let not virtue seek
Remuneration for the thing it was. For beauty, wit,            17

152 *mail* armor    153 *Take the instant way* seize the present moment's pathway    158 *forthright* straight ahead    162 *the abject rear*
the miserable rearguard

High birth, vigor of bone, desert in service,
Love, friendship, charity, are subjects all
To envious and calumniating time.
One touch of nature makes the whole world kin,
That all with one consent praise newborn gauds,          175
Though they are made and molded of things past,
(And give to dust that is a little gilt
More laud than gilt o'erdusted.)
The present eye praises the present object.
Then marvel not, thou great and complete man,          180
That all the Greeks begin to worship Ajax;
Since things in motion sooner catch the eye
Than what stirs not. The cry went once on thee,
And still it might, and yet it may again,
If thou wouldst not entomb thyself alive          185
And case thy reputation in thy tent;
(Whose glorious deeds, but in these fields of late,
Made emulous missions 'mongst the gods them-
    selves
And drave great Mars to faction.)
ACHILLES.                               Of this my privacy
I have strong reasons.
ULYSSES.                    But 'gainst your privacy          190
The reasons are more potent and heroical.
'Tis known, Achilles, that you are in love
With one of Priam's daughters.
ACHILLES. Ha! Known!
ULYSSES. Is that a wonder?          195
(The providence that's in a watchful state
Knows almost every grain of Pluto's gold)

174 *One touch . . . kin* one specific aspect of human nature links
all mankind in a common relationship   175 *gauds* toys   178 *More
laud than gilt o'erdusted* more praise than gold covered with dust
183 *cry* public opinion   188–89 *emulous . . . faction* envious divisions among the gods themselves and drove great Mars to become
a partisan   193 *one of Priam's daughters* Polyxena   197 *Pluto*
Shakespeare, like many others of his day, seems to treat Pluto, god
of the underworld, and Plutus, god of wealth, as one

Finds bottom in th' uncomprehensive deeps,
Keeps place with thought, and almost like the
    gods,
Do thoughts unveil in their dumb cradles.)                    200
There is a mystery—(with whom relation
Durst never meddle)—in the soul of state,
Which hath an operation more divine
Than breath or pen can give expressure to.
All the commerce that you have had with Troy          205
As perfectly is ours as yours, my lord;
And better would it fit Achilles much
To throw down Hector than Polyxena.
(But it must grieve young Pyrrhus now at home,
When fame shall in our islands sound her trump,)          210
And all the Greekish girls shall tripping sing,
"Great Hector's sister did Achilles win,
But our great Ajax bravely beat down him."
Farewell, my lord; I as your lover speak;
The fool slides o'er the ice that you should break.    215
                                                    [Exit.]
PATROCLUS. To this effect, Achilles, have I moved you.
    A woman impudent and mannish grown
    Is not more loathed than an effeminate man
    In time of action. I stand condemned for this;
    They think my little stomach to the war              220
    And your great love to me restrains you thus.
    Sweet, rouse yourself; and the weak wanton Cupid
    Shall from your neck unloose his amorous fold
    And, like a dewdrop from the lion's mane,
    Be shook to air.
ACHILLES.                Shall Ajax fight with Hector?    225
PATROCLUS. Ay, and perhaps receive much honor by
    him.
ACHILLES. I see my reputation is at stake.
    My fame is shrewdly gored.

198 *uncomprehensive* unfathomable    201 *relation* open report    209
*Pyrrhus* Achilles' son, also called Neoptolemus    228 *shrewdly gored*
seriously pierced

PATROCLUS.                        O, then, beware!
   Those wounds heal ill that men do give themselves.
   (Omission to do what is necessary                                    230
   Seals a commission to a blank of danger;
   And danger, like an ague, subtly taints
   Even then when they sit idly in the sun.)
ACHILLES. Go call Thersites hither, sweet Patroclus.
   I'll send the fool to Ajax and desire him                            235
   T' invite the Troyan lords after the combat
   To see us here unarmed. I have a woman's
     longing,
   An appetite that I am sick withal,
   To see great Hector in his weeds of peace,
   To talk with him and to behold his visage,                           240
   Even to my full of view.

   *Enter Thersites.*

                        A labor saved!
THERSITES. A wonder!
ACHILLES. What?
THERSITES. Ajax goes up and down the field, asking
   for himself.                                                         245
ACHILLES. How so?
THERSITES. He must fight singly tomorrow with Hector,
   and is so prophetically proud of an heroical cudgel-
   ing that he raves in saying nothing.
ACHILLES. How can that be?                                                250
THERSITES. Why, he stalks up and down like a pea-
   cock—a stride and a stand; ruminates like an
   hostess that hath no arithmetic but her brain to set
   down her reckoning; bites his lip with a politic
   regard, as who should say, "There were wit in       255
   this head an 'twould out"; and so there is, but it

---

231 *Seals . . . danger* i.e., binds one to confront unnamed danger as
royal agents were given blank commissions, already sealed, to use
for exactions or arrests    239 *weeds* clothes    245 *himself* i.e., Ajax,
with probable pun on "a jakes" or privy    254-55 *politic regard*
shrewd look

lies as coldly in him as fire in a flint, which will not
show without knocking. The man's undone for-
ever, for if Hector break not his neck i' the combat,
he'll break't himself in vainglory. He knows not    26
me. I said, "Good morrow, Ajax"; and he replies,
"Thanks, Agamemnon." What think you of this
man that takes me for the general? He's grown a
very land-fish, languageless, a monster. A plague*
(of opinion! A man may wear it on both sides like    26
a leather jerkin.)

ACHILLES. Thou must be my ambassador to him, Thersites.

THERSITES. Who, I? Why, he'll answer nobody. He pro-
fesses not answering. Speaking is for beggars; he    27
wears his tongue in's arms. I will put on his
presence; let Patroclus make demands to me, you
shall see the pageant of Ajax.

ACHILLES. To him, Patroclus. Tell him I humbly desire
the valiant Ajax to invite the most valorous Hector    27
to come unarmed to my tent, and to procure safe-
conduct for his person of the magnanimous and
most    illustrious,    six-or-seven-times-honored    cap-
tain-general of the Grecian army, Agamemnon, et
cetera. Do this.    28

PATROCLUS. Jove bless great Ajax!

THERSITES. Hum.

PATROCLUS. I come from the worthy Achilles—

THERSITES. Ha!

PATROCLUS. Who most humbly desires you to invite    28
Hector to his tent——

THERSITES. Hum!

PATROCLUS. And to procure safe-conduct from Agamemnon.

(THERSITES. Agamemnon?    29

PATROCLUS. Ay, my lord.

THERSITES. Ha!

266 *jerkin* close-fitting jacket    271 *put on* imitate

PATROCLUS. What say you to't?)

THERSITES. Good b'wi'you, with all my heart.

PATROCLUS. Your answer, sir.                                            295

THERSITES. If tomorrow be a fair day, by eleven of the
clock it will go one way or other; howsoever, he
shall pay for me ere he has me.

(PATROCLUS. Your answer, sir.

THERSITES. Fare ye well, with all my heart.)             300

ACHILLES. Why, but he is not in this tune, is he?

THERSITES. No, but out of tune thus. What music will
be in him when Hector has knocked out his brains,
I know not; but I am sure none, unless the fiddler
Apollo get his sinews to make catlings on.             305

ACHILLES. Come, thou shalt bear a letter to him
straight.

THERSITES. Let me bear another to his horse, for that's
the more capable creature.

ACHILLES. My mind is troubled, like a fountain stirred,   310
And I myself see not the bottom of it.
                    [Exeunt Achilles and Patroclus.]

THERSITES. Would the fountain of your mind were clear
again, that I might water an ass at it! I had rather
be a tick in a sheep than such a valiant ignorance.
                                                [Exit.]


~§ IV. i §~

[Troy. A street before one of the gates.]


Enter at one door Aeneas, with a torch; at another
    Paris, Deiphobus, Antenor, Diomedes the Gre-
    cian, with torches.

PARIS. See, ho! Who is that there?

DEIPHOBUS.                        It is the Lord Aeneas.

305 catlings strings of catgut    309 capable intelligent

AENEAS. Is the prince there in person?
Had I so good occasion to lie long
As you, Prince Paris, nothing but heavenly business
Should rob my bedmate of my company.
DIOMEDES. That's my mind too. Good morrow, Lord
Aeneas.
PARIS. A valiant Greek, Aeneas; take his hand.
(Witness the process of your speech, wherein
You told how Diomed, a whole week by days,
Did haunt you in the field.)
AENEAS.                          Health to you, valiant sir,          1⁰
(During all question of the gentle truce;
But when I meet you armed, as black defiance
As heart can think or courage execute.
DIOMEDES. The one and other Diomed embraces.
Our bloods are now in calm, and, so long, health!          1
But when contention and occasion meet,
By Jove, I'll play the hunter for thy life
With all my force, pursuit, and policy.
AENEAS. And thou shalt hunt a lion that will fly
With his face backward. In humane gentleness,          2⁰
Welcome to Troy. Now, by Anchises' life,
Welcome indeed! By Venus' hand I swear,
No man alive can love in such a sort
The thing he means to kill more excellently.
DIOMEDES. We sympathize. Jove, let Aeneas live,          2
If to my sword his fate be not the glory,
A thousand complete courses of the sun!
But, in mine emulous honor, let him die
With every joint a wound, and that tomorrow!)
AENEAS. We know each other well.          3⁰

---

IV.i.8 *process* gist   9 *by days* day by day   11 *question of* conversation held within   16 *occasion* opportunity   18 *policy* cunning
21 *Anchises* Aeneas's father   22 *Venus's hand* Venus, Aeneas's mother, was wounded in the hand by Diomedes   25 *sympathize* share the same feeling

DIOMEDES. We do, and long to know each other worse.

PARIS. (This is the most despiteful gentle greeting,
The noblest hateful love, that e'er I heard of.)
What business, lord, so early?

AENEAS. I was sent for to the king; but why, I know
not.                                                                  35

PARIS. His purpose meets you; it was to bring this
Greek
To Calchas' house, and there to render him,
For the enfreed Antenor, the fair Cressid.
Let's have your company; or, if you please,
Haste there before us. I constantly do think—          40
Or rather call my thought a certain knowledge—
My brother Troilus lodges there tonight.
Rouse him and give him note of our approach,
With the whole quality wherefore. I fear
We shall be much unwelcome.

AENEAS.                              That I assure you.      45
Troilus had rather Troy were borne to Greece
Than Cressid borne from Troy.

PARIS.                              There is no help.
The bitter disposition of the time
Will have it so. On, lord; we'll follow you.

AENEAS. Good morrow, all.              Exit Aeneas.     50

PARIS. And tell me, noble Diomed; faith, tell me true,
Even in the soul of sound good-fellowship,
Who, in your thoughts, deserves fair Helen best,
Myself or Menelaus?

DIOMEDES.              Both alike.
He merits well to have her that doth seek her,           55
Not making any scruple of her soilure,
With such a hell of pain and world of charge;
And you as well to keep her that defend her,
Not palating the taste of her dishonor,
With such a costly loss of wealth and friends.           60
He, like a puling cuckold, would drink up

40 *constantly* firmly    44 *quality* substance    57 *charge* cost

The lees and dregs of a flat tamed piece;
You, like a lecher, out of whorish loins
Are pleased to breed out your inheritors.
Both merits poised, each weighs nor less nor more;        6
But he as he, the heavier for a whore.

PARIS. You are too bitter to your countrywoman.

DIOMEDES. She's bitter to her country! Hear me,
    Paris—
For every false drop in her bawdy veins
A Grecian's life hath sunk; for every scruple        7
Of her contaminated carrion weight
A Troyan hath been slain. Since she could speak,
She hath not given so many good words breath
As for her, Greeks and Troyans suffered death.

PARIS. Fair Diomed, you do as chapmen do,        7
Dispraise the thing that you desire to buy;
But we in silence hold this virtue well,
We'll not commend what we intend to sell.
Here lies our way.                        *Exeunt.*


#### ◄§ IV. ii §►

[*Troy. Calchas' house. A bedroom and an antechamber.*]


*Enter Troilus and Cressida.*

TROILUS. Dear, trouble not yourself; the morn is cold.

CRESSIDA. Then, sweet my lord, I'll call mine uncle
    down;
He shall unbolt the gates.

TROILUS.                        Trouble him not;
    To bed, to bed. Sleep kill those pretty eyes,

62 *flat tamèd piece* cask opened so long that the wine has gone flat,
hence a stale piece of flesh        65 *poised* weighed        66 *heavier for a
whore* a whore is a loose, i.e., "light" woman, hence adds no weight
70 *scruple* the smallest unit of weight        75 *chapmen* merchants
IV.ii.4 *kill* overpower

And give as soft attachment to thy senses                    5
As infants' empty of all thought!
CRESSIDA.                              Good morrow then.
TROILUS. I prithee now, to bed.
CRESSIDA.                    Are you aweary of me?
TROILUS. O Cressida! But that the busy day,
   Waked by the lark, hath roused the ribald crows,
   And dreaming night will hide our joys no longer,         10
   I would not from thee.
CRESSIDA.                Night hath been too brief.
TROILUS. Beshrew the witch! With venomous wights
      she stays
   As tediously as hell, but flies the grasps of love
   With wings more momentary-swift than thought.
   You will catch cold and curse me.
CRESSIDA.                              Prithee, tarry;      15
   You men will never tarry.
   O foolish Cressid! I might have still held off,
   And then you would have tarried. Hark, there's one
      up.
PANDARUS. [Within] What's all the doors open here?
TROILUS. It is your uncle.                                  20
CRESSIDA. A pestilence on him! Now will he be mock-
      ing.
   I shall have such a life.

   *Enter Pandarus.*

PANDARUS. How now, how now! How go maidenheads?
   Here, you maid, where's my cousin Cressid?
CRESSIDA. Go hang yourself, you naughty mocking
      uncle.                                                25
   You bring me to do, and then you flout me too.
PANDARUS. To do what? To do what? Let her say what.
   What have I brought you to do?
CRESSIDA. Come come; beshrew your heart! You'll
      ne'er be good,
   Nor suffer others.                                       30

12 *venomous wights* evil creatures

PANDARUS. Ha, ha! Alas, poor wretch! A poor capoc-
chia! Hast not slept tonight? Would he not, a
naughty man, let it sleep? A bugbear take him!
CRESSIDA. Did not I tell you? Would he were knocked
i' the head!                                    *One knocks.*
Who's that at door? Good uncle, go and see.       3
My lord, come you again into my chamber.
You smile and mock me, as if I meant naughtily.
TROILUS. Ha, ha!
CRESSIDA. Come, you are deceived, I think of no such
thing.                                          *Knock.*
How earnestly they knock! Pray you, come in.      4
I would not for half Troy have you seen here.
                          *Exeunt [Troilus and Cressida].*
PANDARUS. Who's there? What's the matter? Will you
beat down the door? How now, what's the matter?

    [*Enter Aeneas.*]

AENEAS. Good morrow, lord, good morrow.
PANDARUS. Who's there? My Lord Aeneas! By my
troth,                                          4
I knew you not. What news with you so early?
AENEAS. Is not Prince Troilus here?
PANDARUS. Here? What should he do here?
AENEAS. Come, he is here, my lord. Do not deny him.
It doth import him much to speak with me.        5*
PANDARUS. Is he here, say you? 'Tis more than I know,
I'll be sworn. For my own part, I came in late.
What should he do here?
AENEAS. Who! (Nay, then.) Come, come, you'll do him
wrong ere you are ware. You'll be so true to him, to   5
be false to him. Do not you know of him, but yet
go fetch him hither; go.

    *Enter Troilus.*

TROILUS. How now, what's the matter?

31–32 *capocchia* simpleton    50 *doth import* is important to

AENEAS. My lord, I scarce have leisure to salute you,
My matter is so rash. There is at hand　　　　　60
(Paris your brother, and Deiphobus,)
The Grecian Diomed, and our Antenor
Delivered to us; and for him forthwith,
Ere the first sacrifice, within this hour,
We must give up to Diomedes' hand　　　　　65
The Lady Cressida.

TROILUS.　　　　　　　Is it so concluded?

AENEAS. By Priam, and the general state of Troy.
They are at hand and ready to effect it.

TROILUS. How my achievements mock me!
I will go meet them. And, my Lord Aeneas,　　　　70
We met by chance; you did not find me here.

AENEAS. Good, good, my lord; the secrets of nature
Have not more gift in taciturnity.
　　　　　　　　　　Exeunt [Troilus and Aeneas].

PANDARUS. Is't possible? No sooner got but lost? The
devil take Antenor! The young prince will go mad.　75
A plague upon Antenor! I would they had broke 's
neck!

　　Enter Cressida.

CRESSIDA. How now? What's the matter? Who was
here?

PANDARUS. Ah, ah!　　　　　　　　　　　　80

CRESSIDA. Why sigh you so profoundly? Where's my
lord? Gone? Tell me, sweet uncle, what's the matter?

PANDARUS. Would I were as deep under the earth as
I am above!　　　　　　　　　　　　　　85

CRESSIDA. O the gods! What's the matter?

PANDARUS. Pray thee, get thee in. Would thou hadst
ne'er been born! I knew thou wouldst be his death.
O poor gentleman! A plague upon Antenor!

CRESSIDA. Good uncle, I beseech you on my knees,　90
what's the matter?

60 *rash* urgent

PANDARUS. Thou must be gone, wench, thou must be
gone; thou are changed for Antenor. Thou must
to thy father and be gone from Troilus. 'Twill be
his death; 'twill be his bane; he cannot bear it.

CRESSIDA. O you immortal gods! I will not go.

PANDARUS. Thou must.

CRESSIDA. I will not, uncle. I have forgot my father;
I know no touch of consanguinity—
No kin, no love, no blood, no soul so near me    10
As the sweet Troilus. O you gods divine,
Make Cressid's name the very crown of falsehood
If ever she leave Troilus! Time, force, and death,
Do to this body what extremes you can;
But the strong base and building of my love    10
Is as the very center of the earth,
Drawing all things to it. I will go in and weep——

PANDARUS. Do, do.

CRESSIDA. —Tear my bright hair, and scratch my
praisèd cheeks,
Crack my clear voice with sobs, and break my    10
heart
With sounding Troilus. I will not go from Troy.
                                        *Exeunt.*


## ◄§ IV. iii §►

[*Troy. Before Calchas' house.*]


*Enter Paris, Troilus, Aeneas, Deiphobus, Antenor,
Diomedes.*

PARIS. It is great morning, and the hour prefixed
For her delivery to this valiant Greek
Comes fast upon. Good my brother Troilus,

95 *bane* destruction   99 *consanguinity* blood tie   IV.iii.1 *great
morning* broad daylight

Tell you the lady what she is to do,
And haste her to the purpose.
TROILUS.                          Walk into her house.    5
I'll bring her to the Grecian presently;
And to his hand when I deliver her,
Think it an altar, and thy brother Troilus
A priest there off'ring to it his own heart.
PARIS. I know what 'tis to love;                          10
And would, as I shall pity, I could help.
Please you walk in, my lords.              *Exeunt.*


    ✥§ I V .  i v  §✥

[*Troy. Within Calchas' house.*]


    *Enter Pandarus and Cressida.*

PANDARUS. Be moderate, be moderate.
CRESSIDA. Why tell you me of moderation?
The grief is fine, full, perfect, that I taste,
(And violenteth in a sense as strong
As that which causeth it.) How can I moderate it?    5
(If I could) temporize* with my affections,
(Or brew it to a weak and colder palate,
The like allayment could I give my grief.)
My love admits no qualifying dross;
No more my grief, in such a precious loss.            10

    *Enter Troilus.*

PANDARUS. Here, here, here he comes. Ah, sweet
ducks!
CRESSIDA. O Troilus! Troilus!
PANDARUS. What a pair of spectacles is here! Let me
embrace too. "O heart," as the goodly saying is—    15
    O heart, heavy heart,
    Why sigh'st thou without breaking?

6 *presently* at once   IV.iv.4 *violenteth* rages   9 *dross* impurity

      where he answers again,
            Because thou canst not ease thy smart
            By friendship nor by speaking.             20
There was never a truer rhyme. Let us cast away
nothing, for we may live to have need of such a
verse. We see it, we see it. How now, lambs!
TROILUS. Cressid, I love thee in so strained a purity,
      That the blest gods, as angry with my fancy,         25
      (More bright in zeal than the devotion which
      Cold lips blow to their deities,) take thee from me.
CRESSIDA. Have the gods envy?
PANDARUS. Ay, ay, ay, ay, 'tis too plain a case.
CRESSIDA. And is it true that I must go from Troy?      30
TROILUS. A hateful truth.
CRESSIDA.                  What, and from Troilus too?
TROILUS. From Troy and Troilus.
CRESSIDA.                 Is't possible?
TROILUS. And suddenly, (where injury of chance
      Puts back leave-taking, justles roughly by
      All time of pause, rudely beguiles our lips         35
      Of all rejoindure, forcibly prevents
      Our locked embrasures, strangles our dear vows
      Even in the birth of our own laboring breath.)
      We two, that with so many thousand sighs
      Did buy each other, must poorly sell ourselves     40
      With the rude brevity and discharge of one.
      Injurious time now with a robber's haste
      Crams his rich thievery up, he knows not how.
      As many farewells as be stars in heaven,
      With distinct breath and consigned kisses to them,   45
      He fumbles up into a loose adieu,
      And scants us with a single famished kiss,
      Distasted with the salt of broken tears.
AENEAS. *Within.* My lord, is the lady ready?

24 *strained* filtered   25 *fancy* love   33 *injury of chance* fortuitous
accident   36 *rejoindure* joining again   45–46 *With distinct . . .
adieu* with separate sigh and committed kisses for each farewell, he
clumsily wraps up in a careless adieu   48 *Distasted* the taste de-
stroyed

TROILUS. Hark! You are called. Some say the Genius      50
Cries so to him that instantly must die.
Bid them have patience; she shall come anon.
PANDARUS. Where are my tears? Rain, to lay this wind,
or my heart will be blown up by the root!    [*Exit.*]
CRESSIDA. I must, then, to the Grecians?
TROILUS.                                    No remedy.      55
CRESSIDA. A woeful Cressid 'mongst the merry Greeks!
When shall we see again?
TROILUS. Hear me, love. Be thou but true of heart——
CRESSIDA. I true! How now! What wicked deem is
this?
TROILUS. Nay, we must use expostulation kindly,      60
For it is parting from us.
I speak not "be thou true" as fearing thee,
For I will throw my glove to Death himself
That there's no maculation in thy heart;
But "be thou true," say I, to fashion in      65
My sequent protestation: be thou true,
And I will see thee.
CRESSIDA. O, you shall be exposed, my lord, to dangers
As infinite as imminent; but I'll be true.
TROILUS. And I'll grow friend with danger. Wear this
sleeve.      70
CRESSIDA. And you this glove. When shall I see you?
TROILUS. I will corrupt the Grecian sentinels,
To give thee nightly visitation.
But yet, be true.
CRESSIDA.                O heavens! "Be true" again!
TROILUS. Hear why I speak it, love.      75
The Grecian youths are full of quality;
They're loving, well composed with gift of nature,
And swelling o'er with arts and exercise.

---

50 *Genius* guardian spirit    59 *deem* censorious thought    63 *throw
my glove* give challenge    64 *maculation* taint, i.e., of disloyalty
65–66 *to fashion . . . protestation* to contrive an opening for my
promise to follow    76 *quality* good qualities    78 *arts and exercise*
i.e., theory and practice

(How novelty may move, and parts with person,)
Alas! A kind of godly jealousy—                              8
(Which, I beseech you, call a virtuous sin—)
Makes me afeared.
CRESSIDA.                    O heavens, you love me not!
TROILUS. Die I a villain then!
In this I do not call your faith in question
So mainly as my merit. I cannot sing,                        8
Nor heel the high lavolt, nor sweeten talk,
Nor play at subtle games—fair virtues all,
To which the Grecians are most prompt and preg-
    nant;
But I can tell that in each grace of these
There lurks a still and dumb-discoursive devil             9
That tempts most cunningly. But be not tempted.
CRESSIDA. Do you think I will?
TROILUS. No!
But (something may be done that we will not;
And) sometimes we are devils to ourselves                  95
When we will tempt the frailty of our powers,
Presuming on their changeful potency.
AENEAS. Within. Nay, good my lord!
TROILUS.                           Come, kiss; and
    let us part.
PARIS. Within. Brother Troilus!
TROILUS.                         Good brother, come
    you hither;
And bring Aeneas and the Grecian with you.                100
CRESSIDA. My lord, will you be true?
TROILUS. Who? I? Alas, it is my vice, my fault.
Whiles others fish with craft for great opinion,
I with great truth catch mere simplicity;
(Whilst some with cunning gild their copper crowns,       105
With truth and plainness I do wear mine bare.)

79 *parts with person* accomplishments with personal charm   86
*lavolt* lively dance   88 *pregnant* ready   90 *dumb-discoursive* silent-
speaking   97 *changeful potency* power capable of bringing about
change   103 *opinion* reputation

Fear not my truth; the moral of my wit
Is "plain and true"—there's all the reach of it.

[*Enter Aeneas, Paris, Antenor, Deiphobus and Diomedes.*]

Welcome, Sir Diomed. Here is the lady
Which for Antenor we deliver you.                            110
At the port, lord, I'll give her to thy hand,
And by the way possess thee what she is.
Entreat her fair; and, by my soul, fair Greek,
If e'er thou stand at mercy of my sword,
Name Cressid, and thy life shall be as safe                 115
As Priam is in Ilion.

DIOMEDES.              Fair Lady Cressid,
So please you, save the thanks this prince expects.
The luster in your eye, heaven in your cheek,
Pleads you fair usage; and to Diomed
You shall be mistress, and command him wholly.              120

TROILUS. Grecian, thou dost not use me courteously,
To shame the seal of my petition to thee
In praising her. I tell thee, lord of Greece,
She is as far high-soaring o'er thy praises
As thou unworthy to be called her servant.                  125
I charge thee use her well, even for my charge;
For, by the dreadful Pluto, if thou dost not,
Though the great bulk Achilles be thy guard,
I'll cut thy throat.

DIOMEDES.              O, be not moved, Prince Troilus.
Let me be privileged by my place and message             130
To be a speaker free. When I am hence,
I'll answer to my lust; and know you, lord,
I'll nothing do on charge. To her own worth
She shall be prized; but that you say "be't so,"
I speak it in my spirit and honor, "no."                   135

---

107 *moral* maxim    111 *port* gate of the city    112 *possess* inform
122 *To shame the seal of my petition* to disdain the sealing of my
proposal    126 *even for my charge* simply because I say so    132
*answer to my lust* be responsible to my pleasure

TROILUS. Come, to the port. I'll tell thee, Diomed,
This brave shall oft make thee to hide thy head.
Lady, give me your hand, and, as we walk,
To our own selves bend we our needful talk.

*[Exeunt Troilus, Cressida, and Diomedes.]*
*Sound trumpet.*

PARIS. Hark! Hector's trumpet.
AENEAS.                                How have we spent this
        morning!                                                      140
The prince must think me tardy and remiss,
That swore to ride before him to the field.
PARIS. 'Tis Troilus' fault. Come, come, to field with
        him.
DEIPHOBUS. Let us make ready straight.
AENEAS. Yea, with a bridegroom's fresh alacrity,          145
Let us address to tend on Hector's heels.
The glory of our Troy doth this day lie
On his fair worth and single chivalry.          *Exeunt.*

### ᐊᔆ IV. v ᒃᐁ

*[The Greek camp.]*

*Enter Ajax, armed; Achilles, Patroclus, Agamem-*
*non, Menelaus, Ulysses, Nestor, Calchas, etc.**

AGAMEMNON. Here art thou in appointment fresh and
        fair,
Anticipating time. With starting courage,
Give with thy trumpet a loud note to Troy,
Thou dreadful Ajax, that the appallèd air
May pierce the head of the great combatant          5
And hale him hither.

137 *brave* boast    146 *address* prepare    IV.v.1 *appointment* equip-
ment    2 *starting* active

AJAX.                         Thou, trumpet, there's my
  purse.
  Now crack thy lungs, and split thy brazen pipe.*
  Blow, villain, till thy spheréd bias cheek
  Outswell the colic of puffed Aquilon!*
  Come, stretch thy chest, and let thy eyes spout
    blood;                                                  10
  Thou blow'st for Hector.          [*Trumpet sounds.*]
ULYSSES. No trumpet answers.
ACHILLES.                    'Tis but early days.
AGAMEMNON. Is not yond Diomed with Calchas'
    daughter?
ULYSSES. 'Tis he, I ken the manner of his gait;
  He rises on the toe. That spirit of his               15
  In aspiration lifts him from the earth.

  [*Enter Diomedes, with Cressida.*]

AGAMEMNON. Is this the Lady Cressid?
DIOMEDES.                          Even she.
AGAMEMNON. Most dearly welcome to the Greeks,
    sweet lady.
NESTOR. Our general doth salute you with a kiss.
ULYSSES. Yet is the kindness but particular.           20
  'Twere better she were kissed in general.
NESTOR. And very courtly counsel. I'll begin.
  So much for Nestor.
ACHILLES. I'll take that winter from your lips, fair
    lady.
  Achilles bids you welcome.                           25
MENELAUS. I had good argument for kissing once.
PATROCLUS. But that's no argument for kissing now;
  For thus popped Paris in his hardiment,
  And parted thus you and your argument.
ULYSSES. O, deadly gall, and theme of all our scorns,  30
  For which we lose our heads to gild his horns.

6 *trumpet* trumpeter    8 *bias* puffed-out    9 *Aquilon* the north wind
12 *days* in the day    20 *particular* individual    21 *in general* by
everyone    28 *hardiment* boldness    29 *argument* i.e., Helen

PATROCLUS. The first was Menelaus' kiss; this, mine.
Patroclus kisses you.

MENELAUS.                 O, this is trim.

PATROCLUS. Paris and I kiss evermore for him.

MENELAUS. I'll have my kiss, sir. Lady, by your leave.    35

CRESSIDA. In kissing, do you render or receive?

PATROCLUS. Both take and give.

CRESSIDA.                      I'll make my match to
live,
The kiss you take is better than you give;
Therefore no kiss.

MENELAUS. I'll give you boot; I'll give you three for
one.                                                      40

CRESSIDA. You are an odd man; give even, or give
none.

MENELAUS. An odd man, lady? Every man is odd.

CRESSIDA. No, Paris is not, for you know 'tis true
That you are odd and he is even with you.

MENELAUS. You fillip me o' the head.

CRESSIDA.                         No, I'll be sworn.     45

ULYSSES. It were no match, your nail against his
horn.
May I, sweet lady, beg a kiss of you?

CRESSIDA. You may.

ULYSSES.            I do desire it.

CRESSIDA.                        Why, beg then.

ULYSSES. Why, then, for Venus' sake, give me a kiss,
When Helen is a maid again, and his.                     50

CRESSIDA. I am your debtor; claim it when 'tis due.

ULYSSES. Never's my day, and then a kiss of you.

DIOMEDES. Lady, a word. I'll bring you to your father.
               [*Exeunt Diomedes and Cressida.*]

NESTOR. A woman of quick sense.

ULYSSES.                      Fie, fie upon her!
There's language in her eye, her cheek, her lip;         55

---

37 *I'll . . . to live* I'll bet my life    40 *boot* odds    45 *fillip* tap,
with reference to cuckold's horns

Nay, her foot speaks. Her wanton spirits look out
At every joint and motive of her body.
O, these encounterers, so glib of tongue,
That give a coasting welcome ere it comes,
And wide unclasp the tables of their thoughts          60
To every ticklish reader, set them down
For sluttish spoils of opportunity
And daughters of the game.

*Flourish. Enter all of Troy [Hector, Paris, Aeneas,
Helenus, Troilus, and Attendants].*

ALL. The Troyans' trumpet*
AGAMEMNON.                    Yonder comes the troop.
AENEAS. Hail, all the state of Greece. What shall be
     done                                              65
To him that victory commands? Or do you purpose
A victor shall be known? Will you the knights
Shall to the edge of all extremity
Pursue each other, or shall they be divided
By any voice or order of the field?                    70
Hector bade ask.
AGAMEMNON.      Which way would Hector have it?
AENEAS. He cares not; he'll obey conditions.
AGAMEMNON. 'Tis done like Hector.*
ACHILLES.                    But securely done,
A little proudly, and great deal misprising
The knight opposed.
AENEAS.              If not Achilles, sir,                75
What is your name?
ACHILLES.          If not Achilles, nothing.
AENEAS. Therefore Achilles; but, whate'er, know this:
(In the extremity of great and little,
Valor and pride excel themselves in Hector;
The one almost as infinite as all,                    80

57 *motive* moving part    59 *coasting* sidelong, hence flirtatious    60
*tables* tablets    62 *sluttish spoils of opportunity* whorish plunder of
the passing moment    63 *daughters of the game* prostitutes    73
*securely* overconfidently

The other blank as nothing. Weigh him well;
And that which looks like pride is courtesy.)
This Ajax is half made of Hector's blood,
In love whereof half Hector stays at home;
Half heart, half hand, half Hector comes to seek        85
This blended knight, half Trojan, and half Greek.
ACHILLES. A maiden battle, then? O, I perceive you.

[*Enter Diomedes.*]

AGAMEMNON. Here is Sir Diomed. Go, gentle knight,
Stand by our Ajax. As you and Lord Aeneas
Consent upon the order of their fight,        90
So be it; either to the uttermost,
Or else a breath. The combatants being kin
Half stints their strife before their strokes begin.
(ULYSSES. They are opposed already.)
AGAMEMNON. What Trojan is that same that looks so
heavy?        95
ULYSSES. The youngest son of Priam, a true knight,
(Not yet mature, yet matchless; firm of word,
Speaking in deeds and deedless in his tongue,
Not soon provoked, nor being provoked soon
calmed;
His heart and hand both open and both free,        100
For what he has he gives, what thinks he shows;
Yet gives he not till judgment guide his bounty,
Nor dignifies an impare thought with breath;
Manly as Hector, but more dangerous;
For Hector, in his blaze of wrath, subscribes        105
To tender objects, but he in heat of action
Is more vindicative than jealous love.)
They call him Troilus, and on him erect

---

83 *Hector's blood* as noted, Ajax and Hector are kin        87 *maiden*
beginner's, hence without danger or injury        92 *breath* breathing
space        95 *heavy* heavy-hearted        98 *deedless in his tongue* not
boastful in his speech        100 *free* generous        103 *impare* unworthy
105–106 *subscribes . . . objects* responds to objects capable of
arousing tender emotions

A second hope as fairly built as Hector.
(Thus says Aeneas, one that knows the youth                110
Even to his inches, and with private soul
Did in great Ilion thus translate him to me.)*
                    *Alarum. [Hector and Ajax fight.]*
AGAMEMNON. They are in action.
NESTOR. Now, Ajax, hold thine own!
TROILUS.                               Hector, thou
    sleep'st; awake thee!
AGAMEMNON. His blows are well disposed. There,
    Ajax!                                                115
DIOMEDES. You must no more.    *Trumpets cease.*
AENEAS.                       Princes, enough, so please
    you.
AJAX. I am not warm yet; let us fight again.
DIOMEDES. As Hector pleases.
HECTOR.                     Why, then will I no
    more.
Thou art, great lord, my father's sister's son,
A cousin-german to great Priam's seed;                    120
The obligation of our blood forbids
A gory emulation 'twixt us twain.
(Were thy commixtion Greek and Troyan so
That thou couldst say,) "This hand is Grecian all,
And this is Troyan; the sinews of this leg                125
All Greek, and this all Troy; (my mother's blood
Runs on the dexter cheek, and this sinister
Bounds in my father's," by Jove multipotent,
Thou shouldst not bear from me a Greekish mem-
    ber
Wherein my sword had not impressure made              130
Of our rank feud. But the just gods gainsay
That any drop thou borrow'dst from thy mother,

---

111 *his inches* full height, hence intimately    111 *with private
soul* in confidence    123 *commixtion* composition    127 *dexter* right
127 *sinister* left    128 *multipotent* of many powers

My sacred aunt, should by my mortal sword
Be drained!) Let me embrace thee, Ajax—
By him that thunders, thou hast lusty arms;    135
Hector would have them fall upon him thus.
Cousin, all honor to thee!*

AJAX.                    I thank thee, Hector;
Thou art too gentle and too free a man.
I came to kill thee, cousin, and bear hence
A great addition earnèd in thy death.    140

HECTOR. Not Neoptolemus so mirable,
On whose bright crest Fame with her loud'st
    "Oyes"
Cries, "This is he!" could promise to himself
A thought of added honor torn from Hector.

AENEAS. There is expectance here from both the sides,    145
What further you will do.

HECTOR.                    We'll answer it.
The issue is embracement. Ajax, farewell.

AJAX. If I might in entreaties find success—
As seld I have the chance—I would desire
My famous cousin to our Grecian tents.    150

DIOMEDES. 'Tis Agamemnon's wish; and great Achilles
Doth long to see unarmed the valiant Hector.

HECTOR. Aeneas, call my brother Troilus to me,
And signify this loving interview
To the expecters of our Troyan part.    155
Desire them home. Give me thy hand, my cousin;
I will go eat with thee and see your knights.

[Agamemnon and the rest approach them.]

AJAX. Great Agamemnon comes to meet us here.

HECTOR. The worthiest of them tell me name by name;

---

135 *him that thunders* i.e., Jove    141 *Neoptolemus* usually the name
of Achilles' son, Pyrrhus, but evidently here referring to Achilles
himself    141 *mirable* wonderful    142 *Oyes* cries beginning a herald's proclamation    147 *issue* outcome    149 *seld* seldom    155 *the
expecters of our Troyan part* those Trojans awaiting news    156
*Desire them home* request them return home

But for Achilles, my own searching eyes                160
Shall find him by his large and portly size.
AGAMEMNON. Worthy all arms, as welcome as to one
    That would be rid of such an enemy—
    But that's no welcome. Understand more clear,
    What's past and what's to come is strewed with
        husks                                          165
    And formless ruin of oblivion;
    But in this extant moment, faith and troth,
    (Strained purely from all hollow bias-drawing,)
    Bids thee, with most divine integrity,
    From heart of very heart, great Hector, welcome.   170
HECTOR. I thank thee, most imperious Agamemnon.
AGAMEMNON. [To Troilus] My well-famed lord of
    Troy, no less to you.
MENELAUS. Let me confirm my princely brother's
    greeting.
    You brace of warlike brothers, welcome hither.
HECTOR. Who must we answer?
AENEAS.                    The noble Menelaus.          175
HECTOR. O, you, my lord? By Mars his gauntlet,
    thanks!
    Mock not that I affect th' untraded oath;
    Your quondam wife swears still by Venus' glove.
    She's well, but bade me not commend her to you.
MENELAUS. Name her not now, sir; she's a deadly
    theme.                                             180
HECTOR. O, pardon! I offend.
NESTOR. I have, thou gallant Troyan, seen thee oft,
    Laboring for destiny, make cruel way
    Through ranks of Greekish youth; and I have seen
        thee,
    (As hot as Perseus, spur thy Phrygian steed,       185
    Despising many forfeits and subduements,)

167 *extant* present    168 *bias-drawing* indirectness, hence insincerity
177 *untraded* uncustomary    178 *quondam* former    183 *for destiny*
i.e., as an arm of destiny    186 *Despising many forfeits and subdue-*
*ments* disdaining the victory over those already vanquished and
subdued

When thou hast hung thy advancèd sword i' th'
    air,
Not letting it decline on the declinèd,
That I have said to some my standers-by,
"Lo, Jupiter is yonder, dealing life!"                          190
And I have seen thee pause and take thy breath,
When that a ring of Greeks have shraped thee in,
Like an Olympian wrestling. This have I seen;
But this thy countenance, still locked in steel,
I never saw till now. I knew thy grandsire,                     195
And once fought with him. He was a soldier good;
But, by great Mars, the captain of us all,
Never like thee. O, let an old man embrace thee;
And, worthy warrior, welcome to our tents.

AENEAS. 'Tis the old Nestor.                                    200

HECTOR. Let me embrace thee, good old chronicle,
    That hast so long walked hand in hand with time.
    Most reverend Nestor, I am glad to clasp thee.

NESTOR. I would my arms could match thee in conten-
        tion,
    As they contend with thee in courtesy.                     205

HECTOR. I would they could.

NESTOR. Ha,
    By this white beard, I'd fight with thee tomorrow.
    Well, welcome, welcome. I have seen the time——

ULYSSES. I wonder now how yonder city stands,                   210
    When we have here her base and pillar by us.

HECTOR. I know your favor, Lord Ulysses, well.
    Ah, sir, there's many a Greek and Troyan dead,
    Since first I saw yourself and Diomed
    In Ilion, on your Greekish embassy.                         215

ULYSSES. Sir, I foretold you then what would ensue.
    My prophecy is but half his journey yet;
    For yonder walls, that pertly front your town,
    Yon  towers,  whose  wanton  tops  do  buss  the
        clouds,

187 *hung* held suspended    192 *shraped* hemmed    194 *still* always
195 *grandsire* Laomedon who built the walls of Troy    212 *favor*
face    219 *buss* kiss

Must kiss their own feet.

HECTOR.                    I must not believe you.    220
There they stand yet, and modestly I think,
The fall of every Phrygian stone will cost
A drop of Grecian blood. The end crowns all,
And that old common arbitrator, Time,
Will one day end it.

ULYSSES.                    So to him we leave it.    225
Most gentle and most valiant Hector, welcome.
After the general, I beseech you next
To feast with me and see me at my tent.

ACHILLES. I shall forestall thee, Lord Ulysses, thou!
Now, Hector, I have fed mine eyes on thee;    230
I have with exact view perused thee, Hector,
And quoted joint by joint.

HECTOR.                    Is this Achilles?

ACHILLES. I am Achilles.

HECTOR. Stand fair, I pray thee; let me look on thee.

ACHILLES. Behold thy fill.

HECTOR.                    Nay, I have done already.    235

ACHILLES. Thou art too brief. I will the second time,
As I would buy thee, view thee limb by limb.

HECTOR. O, like a book of sport thou'lt read me o'er;
But there's more in me than thou understand'st.
Why dost thou so oppress me with thine eye?    240

ACHILLES. Tell me, you heavens, in which part of his
body
Shall I destroy him, whether there, or there, or
there?
That I may give the local wound a name,
And make distinct the very breach whereout
Hector's great spirit flew. Answer me, heavens!    245

HECTOR. It would discredit the blessed gods, proud man,
To answer such a question. Stand again.
Think'st thou to catch my life so pleasantly
As to prenominate in nice conjecture
Where thou wilt hit me dead?

232 *quoted* marked    248 *pleasantly* casually    249 *prenominate in
nice conjecture* name beforehand in precise conjecture

ACHILLES.                          I tell thee, yea.          250

HECTOR. Wert thou an oracle to tell me so,
    I'd not believe thee. Henceforth guard thee well,
    For I'll not kill thee there, nor there, nor there;
    But, by the forge that stithied Mars his helm,
    I'll kill thee everywhere, yea, o'er and o'er.          255
    You wisest Grecians, pardon me this brag.
    His insolence draws folly from my lips;
    But I'll endeavor deeds to match these words,
    Or may I never——

AJAX.                     Do not chafe thee, cousin;
    And you, Achilles, let these threats alone,          260
    Till accident or purpose bring you to't.
    You may have every day enough of Hector,
    If you have stomach. The general state, I fear,
    Can scarce entreat you to be odd with him.

HECTOR. I pray you, let us see you in the field.          265
    We have had pelting wars since you refused
    The Grecians' cause.

ACHILLES.                 Dost thou entreat me, Hector?
    Tomorrow do I meet thee, fell as death;
    Tonight all friends.

HECTOR.                  Thy hand upon that match.

AGAMEMNON. First, all you peers of Greece, go to my
        tent;                                          270
    There in the full convive we. Afterwards,
    As Hector's leisure and your bounties shall
    Concur together, severally entreat him
    To taste your bounties. Let the trumpets blow,
    That this great soldier may his welcome know.          275
            Exeunt [all except Troilus and Ulysses].

TROILUS. My Lord Ulysses, tell me, I beseech you,
    In what place of the field doth Calchas keep?

---

254 *stithied* forged    263 *stomach* inclination    263 *general state*
commanders in council    264 *to be odd with* to engage in combat
with    266 *pelting* petty    268 *fell* savage    271 *convive* feast    273
*severally entreat* individually invite    277 *keep* dwell

ULYSSES. At Menelaus' tent, most princely Troilus.
    There Diomed doth feast with him tonight—
    Who neither looks upon the heaven nor earth,    280
    But gives all gaze and bent of amorous view
    On the fair Cressid.
TROILUS. Shall I, sweet lord, be bound to you so much,
    After we part from Agamemnon's tent,
    To bring me thither?
ULYSSES.                    You shall command me, sir.    285
    But gentle tell me, of what honor was
    This Cressida in Troy? Had she no lover there
    That wails her absence?
TROILUS. O, sir, to such as boasting show their scars
    A mock is due. Will you walk on, my lord?    290
    She was beloved, she loved; she is, and doth;
    But still sweet love is food for fortune's tooth.
                                        *Exeunt.*


        ◄§ V . i §►

[*The Greek camp.*]


    *Enter Achilles and Patroclus.*

ACHILLES. I'll heat his blood with Greekish wine to-
        night,
    Which with my scimitar I'll cool tomorrow.
    Patroclus, let us feast him to the height.

    *Enter Thersites.*

(PATROCLUS. Here comes Thersites.)
ACHILLES.                        How now, thou cur
    of envy!
    Thou crusty batch of nature, what's the news?    5

V.i.5 *batch* bread baked together; perhaps, as Theobald suggested,
the word should be "botch"

THERSITES. Why, thou picture of what thou seemest,
and idol of idiot-worshipers, here's a letter for thee.

ACHILLES. From whence, fragment?

THERSITES. Why, thou full dish of fool, from Troy.

PATROCLUS. Who keeps the tent now?                              1

THERSITES. The surgeon's box or the patient's wound.

PATROCLUS. Well said, adversity, and what needs these
tricks?

THERSITES. Prithee, be silent, boy; I profit not by thy
talk. Thou art said to be Achilles' male varlet.              1

PATROCLUS. Male varlet, you rogue! What's that?

THERSITES. Why, his masculine whore. Now, the rotten
diseases of the south, the guts-griping ruptures,
catarrhs, loads o' gravel in the back, lethargies,
cold palsies, raw eyes, dirt-rotten livers, wheez-           2
ing lungs, bladders full of imposthume, sciaticas,
lime-kilns i'the palm, incurable bone-ache, and
the riveled fee-simple of the tetter, and the like,
take and take again such preposterous discoveries!

PATROCLUS. Why, thou damnable box of envy, thou,            2
what means thou to curse thus?

THERSITES. Do I curse thee?

PATROCLUS. Why, no, you ruinous butt, you whoreson
indistinguishable cur, no.

THERSITES. No? Why art thou then exasperate, thou           3
idle immaterial skein of sleave silk, thou green
sarcenet flap for a sore eye, thou tassel of a
prodigal's purse, thou? Ah, how the poor world is
pestered with such water-flies, diminutives of nature.                                                        3

---

11 *The surgeon's . . . wound* Thersites pretends to understand
Patroclus's "tent" in another sense than intended, i.e., as "a probe
for a wound"   18 *diseases of the south* i.e., venereal diseases
19–20 *gravel . . . palsies* kidney stones, apoplectic strokes, paralysis
of the limbs   21 *imposthume* abscess   22 *lime-kilns* burnings   23
*riveled* wrinkled   23 *tetter* chronic ringworm   24 *preposterous
discoveries* unnatural vices, i.e., the male harlotry of Patroclus   28
*ruinous butt* dilapidated cask   29 *indistinguishable* shapeless   31
*sleave silk* silk floss   32 *sarcenet* fine silk

PATROCLUS. Out, gall!

THERSITES. Finch egg!

ACHILLES. My sweet Patroclus, I am thwarted quite
From my great purpose in tomorrow's battle.
Here is a letter from Queen Hecuba,                    40
A token from her daughter, my fair love,
Both taxing me and gagging me to keep
An oath that I have sworn. I will not break it.
Fall Greeks, fail fame, honor or go or stay,
My major vow lies here; this I'll obey.               45
Come, come, Thersites, help to trim my tent;
This night in banqueting must all be spent.
Away, Patroclus!                    *Exit [with Patroclus].*

THERSITES. With too much blood and too little brain,
these two may run mad; but if with too much brain     50
and too little blood they do, I'll be a curer of madmen. Here's Agamemnon, an honest fellow enough,
and one that loves quails, but he has not so much
brain as ear-wax; and the goodly transformation
of Jupiter there, his brother, the bull, the primi-   55
tive statue and oblique memorial of cuckolds—
a thrifty (shoeing-horn in a chain,)* hanging at his
brother's leg—to what form but that he is, should
wit larded with malice and malice forced with wit
turn him to? To an ass, were nothing; he is both      60
ass and ox. To an ox, were nothing; he is both ox
and ass. To be a dog, a mule, a cat, a fitchew,
a toad, a lizard, an owl, a puttock, or a herring
without a roe, I would not care; but to be Menelaus!
I would conspire against destiny. Ask me not what     65
I would be, if I were not Thersites, for I care not

---

42 *taxing* censuring  42 *gaging* binding  53 *quails* prostitutes  54–
56 *transformation . . . cuckolds* Menelaus is likened to Jupiter,
who assumed the shape of a bull in order to seduce Europa, because both are horned, Jupiter as a bull, Menelaus as a cuckold
57–58 *thrifty shoeing-horn . . . leg* stingy tool depending entirely on
his brother, i.e., Agamemnon  59 *forced* stuffed  62 *fitchew* pole-
cat  63 *puttock* small hawk  66–67 *I care not to be* I'd not care if
I were

to be the louse of a lazar, so I were not Menelaus.
Hey-day, sprites and fires!

*Enter Agamemnon, Ulysses, Nestor, [Hector, Ajax,*
*Troilus, Menelaus,] and Diomedes, with lights.*

AGAMEMNON. We go wrong, we go wrong.
AJAX.                              No, yonder 'tis;
There, where we see the lights.
HECTOR.                    I trouble you.                 70
AJAX. No, not a whit.
ULYSSES.          Here comes himself to guide you.

*Enter Achilles.*

ACHILLES. Welcome, brave Hector; welcome, princes
all.
AGAMEMNON. So now, fair prince of Troy, I bid good
night.
Ajax commands the guard to tend on you.
HECTOR. Thanks and good night to the Greeks' general.   75
MENELAUS. Good night, my lord.
HECTOR. Good night, sweet Lord Menelaus.
THERSITES. [*Aside*] Sweet draught! "Sweet," quoth 'a!
Sweet sink, sweet sewer.
ACHILLES. Good night and welcome both at once, to
those                                                    80
That go or tarry.
AGAMEMNON. Good night.
                    *Exeunt Agamemnon, Menelaus.*
ACHILLES. Old Nestor tarries, and you too, Diomed,
Keep Hector company an hour or two.
DIOMEDES. I cannot, lord; I have important business,    85
The tide whereof is now. Good night, great Hec-
tor.
HECTOR. Give me your hand.
ULYSSES. [*Aside to Troilus*] Follow his torch; he goes
to Calchas' tent.
I'll keep you company.

67 *lazar* leper    78 *draught* privy    79 *sink* cesspool    86 *tide* time

TROILUS. Sweet sir, you honor me.

HECTOR.                              And so, good night.    90
  [*Exeunt Diomedes, then Ulysses and Troilus.*]

ACHILLES. Come, come, enter my tent.
          *Exeunt* [*Achilles, Hector, Ajax, and Nestor*].

THERSITES. That same Diomed's a false-hearted rogue,
  a most unjust knave; I will no more trust him when
  he leers than I will a serpent when he hisses. He
  will spend his mouth and promise like Brabbler    95
  the hound; but when he performs, astronomers
  foretell it. It is prodigious, there will come some
  change. The sun borrows of the moon when Diomed keeps his word. I will rather leave to see
  Hector than not to dog him. They say he keeps a    100
  Troyan drab, and uses the traitor Calchas' tent.
  I'll after—nothing but lechery! All incontinent varlets!                                    [*Exit.*]


          ◆§  V . i i  §◆

[*The Greek camp. Before Calchas' tent.*]


      *Enter Diomed.*

DIOMEDES. What, are you up here, ho? Speak.

      [*Enter Calchas.*]*

CALCHAS. Who calls?

DIOMEDES. Diomed. Calchas, I think. Where's your
  daughter?

CALCHAS. She comes to you.                [*Exit.*]

      *Enter Troilus and Ulysses; [after them Thersites.]*

ULYSSES. Stand where the torch may not discover us.    5

      *Enter Cressid.*

95–96 *Brabbler* babbler(?)  quarrelsome(?)    99 *leave to see* miss
seeing

TROILUS. Cressid comes forth to him.

DIOMEDES. How now, my charge!

CRESSIDA. Now, my sweet guardian! Hark, a word with
you. [*Whispers.*]

TROILUS. Yea, so familiar!

ULYSSES. She will sing any man at first sight.

THERSITES. And any man may sing her, if he can take   10
her cliff; she's noted.

DIOMEDES. Will you remember?

CRESSIDA. Remember? Yes.

DIOMEDES. Nay, but do, then;
And yet your mind be coupled with your words.   15

TROILUS. What shall she remember?

ULYSSES. List!

CRESSIDA. Sweet honey Greek, tempt me no more to
folly.

THERSITES. Roguery!

DIOMEDES. Nay, then——

CRESSIDA. I'll tell you what——   20

DIOMEDES. Foh, foh! Come, tell a pin. You are for-
sworn.

CRESSIDA. In faith, I cannot. What would you have me
do?

THERSITES. A juggling trick—to be secretly open.

DIOMEDES. What did you swear you would bestow on
me?

CRESSIDA. I prithee, do not hold me to mine oath;   25
Bid me do anything but that, sweet Greek.

DIOMEDES. Good night.

TROILUS. Hold, patience!

ULYSSES. How now, Troyan?

CRESSIDA. Diomed——   30

DIOMEDES. No, no, good night; I'll be your fool no
more.

TROILUS. Thy better must.

---

V.ii.11 *cliff* clef, with an obscene pun on "cleft"  11 *noted* her
notes are all set down for any man to read, also she is known as
accommodating  23 *open* i.e., sexually

CRESSIDA.                    Hark, a word in your ear.

TROILUS. O plague and madness!

ULYSSES. You are moved, prince; let us depart, I pray,
(Lest your displeasure should enlarge itself                    35
To wrathful terms.) This place is dangerous;
The time right deadly. I beseech you, go.

TROILUS. Behold, I pray you!

ULYSSES.                    Nay, good my lord, go off;
(You flow to great distraction. Come, my lord.)

TROILUS. I prithee, stay.

ULYSSES.                    You have not patience; come.    40

TROILUS. (I pray you, stay!) By hell, and all hell's tor-
ments, I will not speak a word!

DIOMEDES.                    And so, good night.

CRESSIDA. Nay, but you part in anger.

TROILUS.                    Doth that grieve thee?
O withered truth!

ULYSSES.          How now, my lord!

TROILUS.                    By Jove,
I will be patient.

CRESSIDA.          Guardian! Why, Greek!                    45

DIOMEDES. Foh, foh! Adieu; you palter.

CRESSIDA. In faith, I do not. Come hither once again.

ULYSSES. (You shake, my lord, at something.) Will you
go?*
You will break out.

TROILUS.          She strokes his cheek!

ULYSSES.                    Come, come.

TROILUS. Nay, stay; by Jove, I will not speak a word.    50
(There is between my will and all offenses
A guard of patience. Stay a little while.)

THERSITES. How the devil luxury, with his fat rump
and potato finger, tickles these together. Fry,
lechery, fry!                                                  55

DIOMEDES. But will you, then?

CRESSIDA. In faith, I will, la; never trust me else.

53 *luxury* lechery    54 *potato* regarded as an aphrodisiac

DIOMEDES. Give me some token for the surety of it.

CRESSIDA. I'll fetch you one.                    *Exit.*

ULYSSES. You have sworn patience.

TROILUS.                          Fear me not, my lord;    6o
I will not be myself, nor have cognition
Of what I feel. I am all patience.

*Enter Cressida.*

THERSITES. Now the pledge! Now, now, now!

CRESSIDA. Here, Diomed, keep this sleeve.

TROILUS. O beauty, where is thy faith?

ULYSSES.                          My lord——    65

TROILUS. I will be patient; outwardly I will.

CRESSIDA. You look upon that sleeve; behold it well.
He loved me—O false wench! Give't me again.

DIOMEDES. Whose was't?

CRESSIDA.            It is no matter, now I have't again.
I will not meet with you tomorrow night.    70
I prithee, Diomed, visit me no more.

THERSITES. Now she sharpens. Well said, whetstone!

DIOMEDES. I shall have it.

CRESSIDA.            What, this?

DIOMEDES.                    Ay, that.

CRESSIDA. O, all you gods! O pretty, pretty pledge!
Thy master now lies thinking on his bed    75
Of thee and me, and sighs, and takes my glove,
And gives memorial dainty kisses to it,
As I kiss thee. Nay, do not snatch it from me;
He that takes that doth take my heart withal.

DIOMEDES. I had your heart before; this follows it.    80

TROILUS. I did swear patience.

CRESSIDA. You shall not have it, Diomed; faith, you
shall not;
I'll give you something else.

DIOMEDES. I will have this. Whose was it?

CRESSIDA.                    It is no matter.

---

77 *memorial* i.e., of remembrance

DIOMEDES. Come, tell me whose it was.

CRESSIDA. 'Twas one's that loved me better than you will.

But, now you have it, take it.

DIOMEDES.                          Whose was it?

CRESSIDA. By all Diana's waiting-women yond,
And by herself, I will not tell you whose.

DIOMEDES. Tomorrow will I wear it on my helm,                90
And grieve his spirit that dares not challenge it.

TROILUS. Wert thou the devil, and wor'st it on thy horn,
It should be challenged.

CRESSIDA. Well, well, 'tis done, 'tis past. And yet it is not;
I will not keep my word.

DIOMEDES.                    Why then, farewell;                95
Thou never shalt mock Diomed again.

CRESSIDA. You shall not go. One cannot speak a word
But it straight starts you.

DIOMEDES.               I do not like this fooling.

THERSITES. Nor I, by Pluto; but that that likes not you,
pleases me best.                                            100

DIOMEDES. What, shall I come? The hour?

CRESSIDA.                          Ay, come—
O Jove!—
Do come—I shall be plagued.

DIOMEDES.                   Farewell till then.

CRESSIDA. Good night. I prithee, come.
                              Exit [Diomedes].

Troilus, farewell. One eye yet looks on thee,
But with my heart the other eye doth see.                   105
Ah, poor our sex! This fault in us I find,
The error of our eye directs our mind.
What error leads must err. O, then conclude,
Minds swayed by eyes are full of turpitude.    Exit.


88 Diana's waiting-women the moon's attendants, i.e., the stars   98
straight starts you immediately startles, i.e., angers you   99 likes
not you does not please you   102 plagued punished

THERSITES. A proof of strength she could not publish
    more,                                                    110
    Unless she said, "My mind is now turned whore."
ULYSSES. All's done, my lord.
TROILUS.                        It is.
ULYSSES.                             Why stay we, then?
TROILUS. To make a recordation to my soul
    Of every syllable that here was spoke.
    But if I tell how these two did coact,                   115
    Shall I not lie in publishing a truth?
    (Sith yet there is a credence in my heart,
    An esperance so obstinately strong,
    That doth invert th' attest of eyes and ears,
    As if those organs had deceptious functions,             120
    Created only to calumniate.)
    Was Cressid here?
ULYSSES.              I cannot conjure, Troyan.
TROILUS. She was not, sure.
ULYSSES.                     Most sure she was.
TROILUS. Why, my negation hath no taste of madness.
ULYSSES. Nor mine, my lord. Cressid was here but now.        125
TROILUS. Let it not be believed for womanhood!
    Think we had mothers; do not give advantage
    To stubborn critics, apt without a theme
    For depravation, to square the general sex
    By Cressid's rule. Rather think this not Cressid.        130
ULYSSES. What hath she done, prince, that can soil our
    mothers?
TROILUS. Nothing at all, unless that this were she.
THERSITES. Will 'a swagger himself out on's own eyes?

110 *proof of strength* strong proof    110 *publish more* announce
more clearly    118 *esperance* hope    122 *conjure* raise spirits    126
*for* for the sake of    128–130 *apt . . . rule* quite able, without a
specific illustration of depravity, to measure all womankind by
Cressida's standard of behavior    133 *out on's own eyes* out of his
own eyes, i.e., out of accepting the evidence of his own sight

TROILUS. This she? No, this is Diomed's Cressida.
  If beauty have a soul, this is not she;          135
  If souls guide vows, if vows be sanctimonies,
  If sanctimony be the gods' delight,
  If there be rule in unity itself,
  This was not she. O madness of discourse,
  (That cause sets up with and against itself:      140
  Bifold authority, where reason can revolt
  Without perdition, and loss assume all reason
  Without revolt.) This is, and is not, Cressid.
  Within my soul there doth conduce a fight
  Of this strange nature that a thing inseparate    145
  Divides more wider than the sky and earth;
  (And yet the spacious breadth of this division
  Admits no orifice for a point as subtle
  As Ariachne's broken woof to enter.)
  Instance, O instance, strong as Pluto's gates;    150
  Cressid is mine, tied with the bonds of heaven.
  Instance, O instance, strong as heaven itself;
  The bonds of heaven are slipped, dissolved, and
    loosed,
  And with another knot, five-finger-tied,
  The fractions of her faith, orts of her love,     155
  The fragments, scraps, the bits, and greasy relics
  Of her o'ereaten faith, are given to Diomed.
ULYSSES. May worthy Troilus be half attached
  With that which here his passion doth express?
TROILUS. Ay, Greek! And that shall be divulged well  160

138 *If there . . . unity itself* if there exist the principle that unity
is indivisible   139 *discourse* reason   142 *perdition* destruction, i.e.,
madness   142 *loss* i.e., of trust in the evidence of the senses   144
*conduce* go on   145 *a thing inseparate* indivisible, i.e., Cressida
149 *Ariachne's broken woof* the fine cloth spun by Arachne and de-
stroyed by the jealous Athena; subsequently Athena changed Arachne
into a spider   150 *Instance* proof   154 *five-fingered-tied* tied by
mere human hands   155 *orts* scraps, as of food   157 *o'ereaten*
(1) eaten over, thus leaving scraps(?)  (2) overstuffed, thus vom-
ited(?)   158 *half attached* half so much affected

In characters as red as Mars his heart
Inflamed with Venus. Never did young man fancy
With so eternal and so fixed a soul.
Hark, Greek. Much as I do Cressid love,
So much by weight hate I her Diomed;                    165
That sleeve is mine that he'll bear on his helm;
Were it a casque composed by Vulcan's skill,
My sword should bite it. (Not the dreadful spout
Which shipmen do the hurricano call,
Constringed in mass by the almighty sun,                170
Shall dizzy with more clamor Neptune's ear
In his descent than shall my prompted sword
Falling on Diomed.)

THERSITES. He'll tickle it for his concupy.

TROILUS. O Cressid! O false Cressid! False, false, false!   175
Let all untruths stand by thy stainèd name,
And they'll seem glorious.

ULYSSES.                            O, contain yourself;
Your passion draws ears hither.

*Enter Aeneas.*

AENEAS. I have been seeking you this hour, my lord.
Hector, by this, is arming him in Troy;                  180
Ajax, your guard, stays to conduct you home.

TROILUS. Have with you, prince. My courteous lord,
adieu.
Farewell, revolted fair; and Diomed,
Stand fast, and wear a castle on thy head!

ULYSSES. I'll bring you to the gates.                    185

TROILUS. Accept distracted thanks.

                    *Exeunt Troilus, Aeneas, and Ulysses.*

THERSITES. Would I could meet that rogue Diomed. I
would croak like a raven; (I would bode, I would

167 *casque* helmet    170 *constringed* drawn together    172 *prompted*
ready    174 *He'll tickle it for his concupy* (1)he'll, i.e., Troilus will
be well tickled for his concupiscence, i.e. lust(?)   (2)he'll, i.e.,
Troilus will tickle it, i.e. fight it out with Diomedes for his concupy,
i.e., concubine(?)    182 *Have with you* let's go along    188 *bode*
portend disaster

bode. Patroclus will give me anything for the intelligence of this whore. The parrot will not do  190
more for an almond than he for a commodious
drab.) Lechery, lechery; still wars and lechery;
nothing else holds fashion. A burning devil take
them!                                                      *Exit.*


### ᦞ§ V . iii §ᦞ

[*Troy. Priam's palace.*]


*Enter Hector and Andromache.*

ANDROMACHE. When was my lord so much ungently
     tempered,
   To stop his ears against admonishment?
   Unarm, unarm, and do not fight today.
HECTOR. You train me to offend you; get you in.
   By all the everlasting gods, I'll go.                    5
ANDROMACHE. My dreams will, sure, prove ominous
     to the day.
HECTOR. No more, I say.

   *Enter Cassandra.*

CASSANDRA.                Where is my brother Hector?
ANDROMACHE. Here, sister; armed and bloody in intent.
   Consort with me in loud and dear petition;
   Pursue we him on knees, for I have dreamed            10
   Of bloody turbulence, and this whole night
   Hath nothing been but shapes and forms of
     slaughter.
CASSANDRA. O, 'tis true.
HECTOR.            Ho, bid my trumpet sound.


192 *drab* whore   193 *burning devil* venereal disease   V.iii.4 *train*
tempt   4 *offend* insult   6 *ominous to the day* omens of the day's
events

CASSANDRA. No notes of sally, for the heavens, sweet
   brother.

HECTOR. Be gone, I say; the gods have heard me swear.     15

CASSANDRA. The gods are deaf to hot and peevish
   vows.
   They are polluted offerings, more abhorred
   Than spotted livers in the sacrifice.

ANDROMACHE. O, be persuaded! Do not count it holy
   To hurt by being just. It is as lawful,     20
   For we would give much, to use violent thefts,
   And rob in the behalf of charity.

CASSANDRA. It is the purpose that makes strong the
   vow;
   But vows to every purpose must not hold.
   Unarm, sweet Hector.

HECTOR.                Hold you still, I say.     25
   Mine honor keeps the weather of my fate.
   Life every man holds dear; but the dear man
   Holds honor far more precious-dear than life.

   *Enter Troilus.*

   How now, young man; mean'st thou to fight today?

ANDROMACHE. Cassandra, call my father to persuade.     30
                           *Exit Cassandra.*

HECTOR. No, faith, young Troilus; doff thy harness,
   youth.
   I am today i' the vein of chivalry.
   Let grow thy sinews till their knots be strong,
   And tempt not yet the brushes of the war.
   Unarm thee; go, and doubt thou not, brave boy,     35
   I'll stand today for thee and me and Troy.

TROILUS. Brother, you have a vice of mercy in you,
   Which better fits a lion than a man.

---

16 *peevish* silly     21 *For* because     26 *keeps the weather* keeps to
windward, i.e., the position of advantage     27 *dear* honorable     31
*harness* armor     34 *brushes* encounters     37–38 *vice of mercy . . .
lion* lions were thought to be merciful to those that humbled
themselves

HECTOR. What vice is that? Good Troilus, chide me for
  it.
TROILUS. When many times the captive Grecian falls,    40
  Even in the fan and wind of your fair sword,
  You bid them rise and live.
HECTOR. O, 'tis fair play.
TROILUS.                    Fool's play, by heaven, Hector.
HECTOR. How now? How now?
TROILUS.                    For the love of all the gods,
  Let's leave the hermit pity with our mother,    45
  And when we have our armors buckled on,
  The venomed vengeance ride upon our swords,
  Spur them to ruthful work, rein them from ruth.
HECTOR. Fie, savage, fie!
TROILUS.                    Hector, then 'tis wars.
HECTOR. Troilus, I would not have you fight today.    50
TROILUS. Who should withhold me?
  Not fate, obedience, nor the hand of Mars
  Beck'ning with fiery truncheon my retire;
  Not Priamus and Hecuba on knees,
  Their eyes o'ergallèd with recourse of tears;    55
  Nor you, my brother, with your true sword drawn,
  Opposed to hinder me, should stop my way,
  But by my ruin.

  *Enter Priam and Cassandra.*

CASSANDRA. Lay hold upon him, Priam, hold him fast;
  He is thy crutch. Now if thou lose thy stay,    60
  Thou on him leaning, and all Troy on thee,
  Fall all together.
PRIAM.                    Come, Hector, come; go back.
  Thy wife hath dreamt, thy mother hath had visions,
  Cassandra doth foresee, and I myself
  Am like a prophet suddenly enrapt    65

---

48 *ruthful* lamentable    48 *ruth* pity    53 *truncheon* baton used to
signal the end of a combat between champions    55 *o'ergallèd*
inflamed    55 *recourse* repeated pouring down    60 *stay* prop

To tell thee that this day is ominous.
Therefore, come back.
HECTOR.                    Aeneas is afield;
And I do stand engaged to many Greeks,
Even in the faith of valor, to appear
This morning to them.
PRIAM.                    Ay, but thou shalt not go.          70
HECTOR. I must not break my faith.
You know me dutiful; therefore, dear sir,
Let me not shame respect, but give me leave
To take that course by your consent and voice,
Which you do here forbid me, royal Priam.          75
CASSANDRA. O Priam, yield not to him!
ANDROMACHE.                    Do not, dear father.
HECTOR. Andromache, I am offended with you.
Upon the love you bear me, get you in.
                              *Exit Andromache.*
TROILUS. This foolish, dreaming, superstitious girl
Makes all these bodements.
CASSANDRA.                    O farewell, dear Hector!          80
Look, how thou diest; look, how thy eye turns pale;
Look, how thy wounds do bleed at many vents!
Hark, how Troy roars, how Hecuba cries out,
How poor Andromache shrills her dolors forth!
Behold, distraction, frenzy, and amazement,          85
Like witless antics, one another meet,
And all cry Hector! Hector's dead! O Hector!
TROILUS. Away! Away!
CASSANDRA. Farewell. Yet, soft; Hector, I take my
     leave.                                          '
Thou dost thyself and all our Troy deceive.     *Exit.*     90
HECTOR. You are amazed, my liege, at her exclaim.
Go in and cheer the town. We'll forth and fight;
Do deeds worth praise and tell you them at night.


69 *the faith of valor* the word of honor of a brave man     73 *shame
respect* disgrace the respect due a parent     80 *bodements* fore-
bodings     86 *antics* madmen

PRIAM. Farewell. The gods with safety stand about
thee.            [*Exeunt Priam and Hector.*] *Alarum.*
TROILUS. They are at it, hark. Proud Diomed, believe,    95
I come to lose my arm, or win my sleeve.

    *Enter Pandarus.*

PANDARUS. Do you hear, my lord? Do you hear?
TROILUS. What now?
PANDARUS. Here's a letter come from yond poor girl.
TROILUS. Let me read.                                    100
PANDARUS. A whoreson tisick, a whoreson rascally
tisick so troubles me, and the foolish fortune of
this girl; and what one thing, what another, that I
shall leave you one o' these days; and I have a
rheum in mine eyes too, and such an ache in my    105
bones that, unless a man were cursed, I cannot tell
what to think on't. What says she there?
TROILUS. Words, words, mere words, no matter from
the heart;
Th' effect doth operate another way.
                        [*Tearing the letter.*]
Go, wind to wind, there turn and change together.    110
My love with words and errors still she feeds,
But edifies another with her deeds.            *Exeunt.*


    ◅§  V . iv  §▻

[*The battlefield between Troy and the Greek camp.*]*


[*Alarum.*] *Enter Thersites. Excursions.*

THERSITES. Now they are clapperclawing one another;
I'll go look on. That dissembling abominable varlet,
Diomed, has got that same scurvy doting foolish

101 *tisick* cough

young knave's sleeve of Troy there in his helm. I
would fain see them meet, that that same young    5
Troyan ass, that loves the whore there, might send
that Greekish whoremasterly villain with the sleeve
back to the dissembling luxurious drab, of a sleeveless errand. O'the t'other side, the policy of those
crafty swearing rascals—that stale old mouse-    10
eaten dry cheese, Nestor, and that same dog-fox,
Ulysses—is not proved worth* a blackberry. They
set me up, in policy, that mongrel cur, Ajax,
against that dog of as bad a kind, Achilles. And
now is the cur Ajax prouder than the cur Achilles,    15
and will not arm today. Whereupon the Grecians
begin to proclaim barbarism, and policy grows
into an ill opinion.

*Enter Diomedes and Troilus.*

Soft, here comes sleeve, and t'other.

TROILUS. Fly not; for shouldst thou take the river Styx,    20
I would swim after.

DIOMEDES.                Thou dost miscall retire.
I do not fly, but advantageous care
Withdrew me from the odds of multitude.
Have at thee!

THERSITES. Hold thy whore, Grecian! Now for thy
whore,                                                    25
Troyan! Now the sleeve, now the sleeve!
            [*Exeunt Troilus and Diomedes, fighting.*]

*Enter Hector.*

HECTOR. What art thou, Greek? Art thou for Hector's
match?
Art thou of blood and honor?

---

V.iv.8–9 *sleeveless* futile    10 *crafty swearing* i.e., crafty to the extent of perjury    17–18 *proclaim barbarism . . . opinion* adopt an-
archic barbarity, and organized polity, i.e., government, falls into
disrepute    22–23 *but advantageous . . . of multitude* care for my
own advantage led me to avoid facing heavy odds

THERSITES. No, no, I am a rascal, a scurvy railing
knave, a very filthy rogue.                                        30

HECTOR. I do believe thee; live.                    [*Exit.*]

THERSITES. God-a-mercy, that thou wilt believe me; but
a plague break thy neck—for frighting me. What's
become of the wenching rogues? I think they have
swallowed one another. I would laugh at that mir-      35
acle—yet, in a sort, lechery eats itself. I'll seek
them.                                                         *Exit.*


⋙ V. v ⋘

[*The battlefield.*]


*Enter Diomedes and Servant.*

DIOMEDES. Go, go, my servant, take thou Troilus'
horse;
Present the fair steed to my Lady Cressid.
Fellow, commend my service to her beauty;
Tell her I have chastised the amorous Troyan,
And am her knight by proof.

SERVANT.                          I go, my lord.   [*Exit.*]     5

*Enter Agamemnon.*

AGAMEMNON. Renew, renew! (The fierce Polydamas
Hath beat down Menon;) bastard Margarelon
(Hath Doreus prisoner,
And) stands colossus-wise, waving his beam,
Upon the pashèd corses (of the kings                        10
Epistrophus and Cedius;) Polyxenes is slain,
(Amphimachus and Thoas deadly hurt,)
Patroclus ta'en or slain, (and Palamedes
Sore hurt and bruised.) The dreadful Sagittary

V.v.9 *beam* spear   10 *pashèd corses* battered corpses   14 *Sagittary* a creature half man, half horse who fought for the Trojans he
was a remarkable archer

Appals our numbers. Haste we, Diomed,          15
To reinforcement, or we perish all.

*Enter Nestor.\**

NESTOR. Go, bear Patroclus' body to Achilles,
And bid the snail-paced Ajax arm for shame.
There is a thousand Hectors in the field;
Now here he fights on Galathe his horse,          20
And there (lacks work; anon he's there afoot,
And there they fly or die, like scalèd sculls
Before the belching whale; then is he yonder,
And there) the strawy Greeks, ripe for his edge,
Fall down before him, like a mower's swath.          25
Here, there, and everywhere, he leaves and takes,
Dexterity so obeying appetite
That what he will he does, and does so much
That proof is called impossibility.

*Enter Ulysses.*

ULYSSES. O, courage, courage, princes! Great Achilles          30
Is arming, weeping, cursing, vowing vengeance!
Patroclus' wounds have roused his drowsy blood,
Together with his mangled Myrmidons,
That noseless, handless, hacked and chipped, come
    to him,
Crying on Hector. Ajax hath lost a friend,          35
And foams at mouth, and he is armed and at it,
Roaring for Troilus, (who hath done today
Mad and fantastic execution,
Engaging and redeeming of himself
With such a careless force and forceless care          40
As if that luck, in very spite of cunning,
Bade him win all.)

*Enter Ajax.*

AJAX. Troilus, thou coward Troilus!          *Exit.*

---

22 *scalèd sculls* scaly schools of fish     24 *strawy* like straw     24 *edge*
i.e., of his sword, here compared to a scythe

DIOMEDES.                          Ay, there, there.
NESTOR. (So, so,)* we draw together.            *Exit.*

*Enter Achilles.*

ACHILLES.                     Where is this Hector?
Come, come, thou boy-queller, show thy face;          45
Know what it is to meet Achilles angry.
Hector, where's Hector? I will none but Hector.
                                        *Exit.*


        ❦ V. vi ❧

[*The battlefield.*]


    *Enter Ajax.*

AJAX. Troilus, thou coward Troilus, show thy head!

    *Enter Diomedes.*

DIOMEDES. Troilus, I say, where's Troilus?
AJAX.                         What wouldst thou?
DIOMEDES. I would correct him.
AJAX. Were I the general, thou shouldst have my office
    Ere that correction. Troilus, I say! What, Troilus!     5

    *Enter Troilus.*

TROILUS. O traitor Diomed! Turn thy false face, thou
    traitor,
    And pay thy life thou owest me for my horse.
DIOMEDES. Ha, art thou there?
AJAX. I'll fight with him alone. Stand, Diomed.
DIOMEDES. He is my prize; I will not look upon.          10
TROILUS. Come, both you cogging Greeks; have at
    you both!                    [*Exeunt, fighting.*]

45 *boy-queller* boy-killer   V.vi.5 *correction* opportunity to correct,
i.e., administer punishment   10 *look upon* stand by as a spectator
11 *cogging* deceitful

*Enter Hector.*

HECTOR. Yea, Troilus? O, well fought, my youngest
brother!

*Enter Achilles.*

ACHILLES. Now do I see thee, ha! Have at thee,
   Hector!                [*They fight; Achilles tires.*]
HECTOR. Pause, if thou wilt.
ACHILLES. I do disdain thy courtesy, proud Troyan;        15
   Be happy that my arms are out of use.
   My rest and negligence befriends thee now,
   But thou anon shalt hear of me again;
   Till when, go seek thy fortune.                *Exit.*
HECTOR.                        Fare thee well;
   I would have been much more a fresher man,               20
   Had I expected thee.

   (*Enter Troilus.*

                        How now, my brother!
TROILUS. Ajax hath ta'en Aeneas! Shall it be?
   No, by the flame of yonder glorious heaven,
   He shall not carry him; I'll be ta'en too,
   Or bring him off. Fate, hear me what I say!             25
   I reck not though thou end my life today.       *Exit.*)

   *Enter one in armor.*

HECTOR. Stand, stand, thou Greek; thou art a goodly
   mark.
   No? Wilt thou not? I like thy armor well;
   I'll frush it and unlock the rivets all,
   But I'll be master of it. Wilt thou not, beast, abide?   30
   Why then, fly on, I'll hunt thee for thy hide.
                        *Exit* [*in pursuit*].

---

22 *ta'en* taken, i.e., captive    24 *carry him* i.e., off, as a captive
29 *frush it* strike it violently

## ᵔᵍ V . v i i ᶜᵕ

[*The battlefield.*]

*Enter Achilles with Myrmidons.*

ACHILLES. Come here about me, you my Myrmidons;
Mark what I say. Attend me where I wheel.
Strike not a stroke, but keep yourselves in breath.
And when I have the bloody Hector found,
Empale him with your weapons round about;                      5
In fellest manner execute your arms.
Follow me, sirs, and my proceedings eye;
It is decreed Hector the great must die.
                              *Exit [with Myrmidons].*

*Enter Thersites, Menelaus, Paris [the last two
fighting].*

THERSITES. The cuckold and the cuckold-maker are at
it. Now, bull! Now, dog! Low, Paris, low! Now,      10
my double-horned Spartan! Low, Paris, low! The
bull has the game; 'ware horns, ho!
                              *Exeunt Paris and Menelaus.*

*Enter Bastard [Margarelon].*

BASTARD. Turn, slave, and fight.
THERSITES. What art thou?
BASTARD. A bastard son of Priam's.                              15
THERSITES. I am a bastard too; I love bastards. I am bas-
tard begot, bastard instructed, bastard in mind, bas-

V.vii.5 *Empale him* hem him in   6 *fellest* most savage   6 *execute*
use   10–12 *Now, bull! . . . ho!* Thersites mimicks a spectator at a
bull-baiting held in Paris Garden with the bull, i.e., Menelaus,
attacked by the dog, i.e., Paris, but apparently driving him off with
his cuckold's horns

tard in valor, in everything illegitimate. One bear will
not bite another, and wherefore should one bastard? Take heed, the quarrel's most ominous to us.    20
If the son of a whore fight for a whore, he tempts
judgment. (Farewell, bastard.)

BASTARD. The devil take thee, coward!*    *Exeunt.*


⋖⦆ V . viii ⦆⋗

[*The battlefield.*]


*Enter Hector.*

HECTOR. (Most putrefièd core, so fair without,
    Thy goodly armor thus hath cost thy life.)
    Now is my day's work done; I'll take my breath.
    Rest, sword; thou hast thy fill of blood and death.
                [*Puts off his helmet, and
                hangs his shield behind him.*]

    *Enter Achilles and Myrmidons.*

ACHILLES. Look, Hector, how the sun begins to set,    5
    How ugly night comes breathing at his heels.
    Even with the vail and dark'ning of the sun,
    To close the day up, Hector's life is done.
HECTOR. I am unarmed; forgo this vantage, Greek.
ACHILLES. Strike, fellows, strike. This is the man I seek.    10
                [*Hector falls.*]
    So, Ilion, fall thou next! Come, Troy, sink down!
    Here lies thy heart, thy sinews, and thy bone.
    On, Myrmidons, and cry you all amain,
    "Achilles hath the mighty Hector slain!"    *Retreat.*
    Hark, a retire upon our Grecian part.    15


V.iii.7 *vail* going down

ONE GREEK. The Troyans' trumpets sound the like, my
lord.

ACHILLES. The dragon wing of night o'erspreads the
earth,
And sticklerlike the armies separates.
My half-supped sword, that frankly would have
fed,
Pleased with this dainty bait, thus goes to bed.    20
[*Sheathes his sword.*]
Come, tie his body to my horse's tail;
Along the field I will the Troyan trail.    *Exeunt.*

◄§ V . ix §►

[*The battlefield.*]

*Enter Agamemnon, Ajax, Menelaus, Nestor, Dio-
medes, and the rest, marching. [Sound retreat.
Shout.]*

AGAMEMNON. Hark, hark, what shout is that?
NESTOR.                                    Peace, drums!
SOLDIERS. [*Within*]                              Achilles!
Achilles! Hector's slain! Achilles!
DIOMEDES. The bruit is, Hector's slain, and by
Achilles.
AJAX. If it be so, yet bragless let it be;
Great Hector was as good a man as he.    5
AGAMEMNON. March patiently along. Let one be sent
To pray Achilles see us at our tent.
If in his death the gods have us befriended,
Great Troy is ours, and our sharp wars are ended.
*Exeunt.*

18 *And sticklerlike the armies separates* and umpirelike separates
the armies, i.e., the night does so    19 *frankly* abundantly    V.ix.3
*bruit* rumor

⚜ V . x ⚜

[*The battlefield.*]


*Enter Aeneas, Paris, Antenor, Deiphobus.*

AENEAS. Stand, ho! Yet are we masters of the field.
Never go home; here starve we out the night.

*Enter Troilus.*

TROILUS. Hector is slain.
ALL.                         Hector! The gods forbid!
TROILUS. He's dead and at the murderer's horse's tail,
In beastly sort, dragged through the shameful field.          5
Frown on, you heavens, effect your rage with speed;
Sit, gods, upon your thrones, and smile at Troy.
I say, at once let your brief plagues be mercy,
And linger not our sure destructions on.
AENEAS. My lord, you do discomfort all the host.          10
TROILUS. You understand me not that tell me so.
I do not speak of flight, of fear, of death,
But dare all imminence that gods and men
Address their dangers in. Hector is gone.
Who shall tell Priam so, or Hecuba?          15
Let him that will a screech owl aye be called
Go in to Troy, and say there Hector's dead.
There is a word will Priam turn to stone,
Make wells and Niobes of the maids and wives,
Cold statues of the youth, and in a word          20
Scare Troy out of itself. But march away.

V.x.7 *smile* i.e., in derision    13–14 *But dare . . . dangers in* but
dare whatever imminent dangers gods and men may be preparing
19 *Niobes* ever-weeping columns of stone; after the death of her
seven sons and seven daughters the wailing Niobe was changed into
stone from which tears continued to flow

Hector is dead; there is no more to say.
Stay yet. You vile abominable tents,
Thus proudly pitched upon our Phrygian plains,
Let Titan rise as early as he dare,                        25
I'll through and through you! And, thou great-sized
  coward,
No space of earth shall sunder our two hates.
I'll haunt thee like a wicked conscience still,
That moldeth goblins swift as frenzy's thoughts.
Strike a free march to Troy. With comfort go;             30
Hope of revenge shall hide our inward woe.

*Enter Pandarus.*

PANDARUS. But hear you, hear you!
TROILUS. Hence, broker, lackey! Ignominy and shame
  Pursue thy life, and live aye with thy name.
                         *Exeunt all but Pandarus.*
PANDARUS. A goodly medicine for my aching bones! O    35
  world, world! Thus is the poor agent despised. O
  traders and bawds, how earnestly are you set
  awork, and how ill requited! Why should our en-
  deavor be so loved, and the performance so
  loathed? What verse for it? What instance for it?    40
  Let me see.
     Full merrily the humble-bee doth sing,
     Till he hath lost his honey and his sting;
     And being once subdued in armèd tail,
     Sweet honey and sweet notes together fail.        45
  Good traders in the flesh, set this in your painted
     cloths:
  "As many as be here of Pandar's hall,
  Your eyes, half out, weep out at Pandar's fall;
  Or if you cannot weep, yet give some groans,
  Though not for me, yet for your aching bones."        50

---

25. *Titan* i.e., Helios, the sun, who was one of the Titans    26
*coward* i.e., Achilles    46 *painted cloths* painted cloth hangings,
found in brothels

Brethren and sisters of the hold-door trade,
Some two months hence my will shall here be
    made.
It should be now, but that my fear is this,
Some gallèd goose of Winchester would hiss.
Till then I'll sweat and seek about for eases,                55
And at that time bequeath you my diseases.

[*Exit.*]

F I N I S

51 *hold-door trade* prostitution    54 *gallèd goose of Winchester*
probably a prostitute with venereal disease; the brothels of South-
wark were under the jurisdiction of the Archbishop of Winchester,
hence a Winchester goose was a prostitute    55 *sweat* a treatment
for venereal disease

# Production Notes

PROLOGUE    *Enter the Prologue in armor.* The director used the Prologue to set the tone of the play. Clad in armor, he was fat, jolly, and bearded. Good natured and pleasant, he doubled as Cressida's man, Alexander; serving as her confidant as well as a court gossip. Although beginning the opening speech at a heroic level, he gradually lowered the tone through a suggestive and lascivious manner of delivery.

I. i.    Neither Quarto nor Folio contains act-scene divisions. The present divisions, established by early editors and hallowed by tradition, are introduced for the convenience of the reader. On the Delacorte Theater stage, the action was continuous, save for an intermission after III. ii.

   4    *Troyans* Throughout the text the warriors of Troy are called Troyans. In the Festival production conventional pronunciation was observed, Troyan being pronounced Trojan.

   63    *But, saying* "And doing" was substituted to provide transition required by stage cutting. Occasionally the alteration of the text necessitated additions or substitutions to accommodate the sense. These changes are noted below.

   108    s.d. *Enter Aeneas.* Antenor, Deiphobus, and Margarelon enter with Aeneas. On sound of alarum (116), Deiphobus and Margarelon pick up armor previously discarded by Troilus and carry it off stage.

I. ii.  110   *him* "Troilus" was substituted.

    183 Two Trojan soldiers enter Left with tray of goblets for the returning warriors, each of whom enters Right, crosses to the soldiers, drinks, and exits Left. Soldiers exit at 240.

I. iii.  *Before Agamemnon's pavilion.* The scenic focus of the council scene was a model of six-gated Troy to which the leaders referred throughout their discussions.

    61  *most reverend* to "most reverend" was added "Nestor"

  179  *abilities, gifts* to which were added "orders, plots"

  214  s.d. *Enter Aeneas.* The exchange between Agamemnon and Aeneas was played for its comic values. During performances audience laughter occurred at the ends of lines 222, 234, 249, 254, and after the word "himself" in line 256.

II. ii.  The principal stage property used in this scene was a throne, platform center, in which Priam sat during the first part of the debate.

  162  In the Festival production Priam left the stage at the end of Paris's speech.

  189  During rehearsals attempts were made to motivate Hector's change of heart, but the suddenness of the change made these attempts futile. The actor had to play Hector's about-face forthrightly and without apology.

II. iii.  35   *lazars* "lepers" substituted

III. i.  138   *He . . . something.* Helen addressed the line to Paris, "he" referring to Pandarus.

III. ii.  22   *Sounding* "swooning" substituted

  101  s.d. *Enter Pandarus.* He entered carrying pillows.

  213  s.d. *Exit.* The single intermission occurred at this point in the play.

III. iii. 23–25   The lines were conflated to read "is such a man that they will almost"

57ff.   The Greek leaders, who were downstage on the platform, now cross upstage and pass before the entrance to Achilles' tent.

104–110   Lines were conflated to read:
> The bearer knows not, till it travels forth
> To be thus mirrored in another's eyes.

Although the word "married" appears both in Quarto and all Folio copies, scholars have generally accepted the emendation "mirrored."

264   A plague of opinion! altered to "A plague upon him!"

IV. iv. 6   If I could temporize . . . altered to "Can I temporize . . ."

IV. v. s.d. Enter Ajax . . . Although Quarto and Folios include Calchas among the characters on stage, Diomedes takes Cressida off stage to meet her father, suggesting that the text is in error and that Calchas should not be in this scene, a practice followed by the Festival production.

7, 9   At the conclusion of these lines, additional trumpet calls were inserted for comic effect.

64   The Troyans' trumpet. This line was given to Menelaus.

73–75   This speech is assigned to Agamemnon in the Quarto and Folios. However, from Aeneas's address to Achilles, which follows, it is evident that at least the last part of the speech belongs to Achilles. Theobald (1733 edition) was the first to note the difficulty, but remedied the matter by giving the entire speech to Achilles. A more satisfactory arrangement, widely accepted, is the one adopted by the Festival and reproduced in the present text.

112   Ulysses' line "They are opposed already" (94) was advanced to this point. The fight itself did not employ lists and consisted of a contest with quarter staffs.

119–137  The Festival cutting actually reverses the meaning of the speech so that Hector seems to state that he *can* distinguish between a hand that is "Grecian all" and one that is "Troyan all." However, the cutting permitted an ironic delivery that conveyed the original idea in a less obvious manner.

V. i. 57  *shoeing-horn in a chain* "tool" substituted

V. ii. 1 s.d.  [*Enter Calchas.*] Editors usually mark Calchas's lines as being spoken "within." In the Festival production, Calchas made an entrance.
48  *You shake, my lord, at something. Will you go?* altered to "Will you go, my lord"

V. iv.–x.  These scenes are continuous. The divisions adopted by earlier editors are maintained for convenience of reference but do not indicate any suspension of action. For the battlefield scenes, battering rams were strewn over the stage platform.

V. iv. 12  *is not proved worth* altered to "is proved not worth"

V. v. 16 s.d.  *Enter Nestor.* Patroclus's body is borne on stage. Soldiers obey Nestor as he bids them, "Go, bear Patroclus' body to Achilles."

V. v. 44  *So, so* altered to "now, now,"

V. vii. 21–23  *he tempts . . . coward!* Sequence altered as follows:

> . . . he tempts judgment.
> *Bastard.* The devil take thee, coward!
> *Thersites.* Farewell, bastard.
>                              *Exeunt.*

# Reference List

RECENT EDITIONS OF *Troilus and Cressida*

A New Variorum Edition, ed. Harold N. Hillebrand. Supplemental ed. T. W. Baldwin (Philadelphia: J. B. Lippincott Co., 1953).

The Yale Shakespeare Edition, ed. Jackson J. Campbell. (New Haven: Yale University Press, 1956).

The New Cambridge Edition, ed. Alice Walker. (Cambridge, England: Cambridge University Press, 1957).

The Pelican Shakespeare, ed. Virgil K. Whitaker. (Baltimore: Penguin Books, 1958).

The Signet Classic Shakespeare, ed. Daniel Seltzer. (New York: New American Library, 1963).

BOOKS AND ARTICLES ABOUT *Troilus and Cressida*

Alexander, Peter. "*Troilus and Cressida*, 1609," *Library*, IX. (1928), 267–86.

Almeida, Barbara Heliodora C. de M. F. de. "*Troilus and Cressida*: Romantic Love Revisited," *Shakespeare Quarterly*, XV. (1964), 327–32.

Boas, G. "*Troilus and Cressida* and the Time Scheme," *New English Review*, XIII. (1946), 529–35.

Bowden, William R. "The Human Shakespeare and *Troilus and Cressida*," *Shakespeare Quarterly*, VIII. (1957), 167–77.

Bradbrook, M. C. "What Shakespeare did to Chaucer's *Troilus and Criseyde*," *Shakespeare Quarterly*, IX. (1958), 311–19.

Brooke, C. F. Tucker. "Shakespeare's Study in Culture and Anarchy," *Yale Review*, XVII. (1928), 571–77.

Campbell, Oscar J. *Comicall Satyre and Shakespeare's Troilus and Cressida* (San Marino, Calif.: Huntington Library Publications, 1938).

208     REFERENCE LIST

Charlton, H. B. "The Dark Comedies," *Bulletin of the John Rylands Library*, XXI. (1937), 78–128.

Daniels, F. Q. "Order and Confusion in *Troilus and Cressida*, I.iii." *Shakespeare Quarterly*, XII. (1961), 285–91.

Ellis-Fermor, Una. " 'Discord in the Spheres': The Universe of *Troilus and Cressida*," *The Frontiers of the Drama* (London: Methuen & Co. Ltd., 1945), 2nd ed. 1964.

Foakes, R. A. "*Troilus and Cressida* Reconsidered," *University of Toronto Quarterly*, XXXII. (1963), 142–54.

Gerard, Albert. "Meaning and Structure in *Troilus and Cressida*," *English Studies*, XL. (1959), 148–51, 156–57.

Greg, W. W. "The Printing of Shakespeare's *Troilus and Cressida* in the First Folio," *Papers of the Bibliographical Society of America*, XLV. (1951), 273–82.

Harrier, R. C. "Troilus Divided," in *Studies in the English Renaissance Drama in memory of K. J. Holzknecht* (New York: New York University Press, 1959), 142–56.

Hotson, Leslie. "Love's Labour's Won," *Shakespeare Sonnets Dated* (New York: Oxford University Press, 1949).

Kaula, David. "Will and Reason in *Troilus and Cressida*," *Shakespeare Quarterly*, XII. (1961), 271–83.

Kimbrough, Robert. *Shakespeare's Troilus & Cressida and Its Setting* (Cambridge, Mass.: Harvard University Press, 1964).

Knowland, A. S. "*Troilus and Cressida*," *Shakespeare Quarterly*, X. (1959), 353–65.

Kott, Jan. *Shakespeare our Contemporary*. tr. Boleslaw Taborski (Garden City, N.Y., Doubleday & Co., Inc., 1964).

Lawrence, William W. *Shakespeare's Problem Comedies*. (New York: The Macmillan Company, 1931).

Main, W. W. "Character Amalgams in Shakespeare's *Troilus and Cressida*," *Studies in Philology*, LVIII. (1961), 170–8.

Morris, B. R. "The Tragic Structure of *Troilus and Cressida*," *Shakespeare Quarterly*, X. (1959), 481–91.

Reynolds, George F. "*Troilus and Cressida* on the Elizabethan Stage," *Joseph Quincy Adams Memorial Studies*, ed. J. G. McManaway, G. E. Dawson, E. E. Willoughby. (Washington, D.C., Folger Shakespeare Library, 1948).

Rollins, Hyder E. "The Troilus-Cressida Story from Chaucer to Shakespeare," *Publications of the Modern Language Association*, XXXII. (1917), 383–429.

Sewell, Arthur. "Notes on the Integrity of *Troilus and*

Cressida," *Review of English Studies*, XIX. (1943), 120–27.

Tillyard, E. M. W. *Shakespeare's Problem Plays* (Toronto: University of Toronto Press, 1950).

Walker, Alice. *Textual Problems of the First Folio*. (New York and London: Cambridge University Press, 1953).

Williams, Philip. "Shakespeare's *Troilus and Cressida*: The Relationship of Quarto and Folio," in *Studies in Bibliography*, III (Charlottesville, Virginia: Bibliographical Society of the University of Virginia, 1950), 131–43.

# Appendix:

# Preface to 1609 Quarto

*A Never Writer, to an Ever Reader. News.*

Eternal reader, you have here a new play, never staled
with the stage, never clapperclawed with the palms of
the vulgar, and yet passing full of the palm comical; for
it is a birth of your brain, that never undertook anything comical vainly. And were but the vain names of
comedies changed for the titles of commodities, or of
plays for pleas, you should see all those grand censors,
that now style them such vanities, flock to them for the
main grace of their gravities—especially this author's
comedies, that are so framed to the life that they serve
for the most common commentaries of all the actions
of our lives, showing such a dexterity and power of wit
that the most displeased with plays are pleased with his
comedies. And all such dull and heavy-witted worldlings
as were never capable of the wit of a comedy, coming
by report of them to his representations, have found
that wit there that they never found in themselves, and
have parted better witted than they came, feeling an
edge of wit set upon them, more than ever they dreamed
they had brain to grind it on. So much and such savored
salt of wit is in his comedies that they seem, for their
height of pleasure, to be born in that sea that brought
forth Venus. Amongst all there is none more witty than
this. And had I time I would comment upon it, though
I know it needs not, for so much as will make you think
your testern well bestowed, but for so much worth as
even poor I know to be stuffed in it. It deserves such a
labor as well as the best comedy in Terence or Plautus.
And believe this, that when he is gone, and his comedies

out of sale, you will scramble for them, and set up a new English Inquisition. Take this for a warning, and at the peril of your pleasure's loss, and judgment's, refuse not, nor like this the less for not being sullied with the smoky breath of the multitude; but thank fortune for the 'scape it hath made amongst you, since by the grand possessors' wills I believe you should have prayed for them rather than been prayed. And so I leave all such to be prayed for (for the state of their wits' healths) that will not praise it. *Vale*.